HOW THEY SELL MUSIC

LESSONS BY

Bubba Sparxxx Cody Canada DJ DU
Adley Stump Andrew Belle Lisa Lavie
Mister Billy Jef Jon Sin Thick As Thieves
Peter Hollens Cimorelli The Cab

How They Sell Music Publishing • Nashville, TN

Published by:

HOW THEY SELL MUSIC PUBLISHING
1109 16th Ave S.
Nashville, TN 37212
www.HowTheySellMusic.com

First Printing, 2015

ISBN: 978-0-9863738-0-0
ISBN: 978-0-9863738-1-7 (Kindle)
ISBN: 978-0-9863738-2-4 (Other eReaders)
LCCN: 2015905036

Ordering Information:

Quantity sales. Special discounts are available on quantity purchases by corporations, associations, and others. For details, contact the "Special Sales Department" at the address above.

Printed in the United States of America

21 20 19 18 17 16 15 10 9 8 7 6 5 4 3 2 1

*How They Sell Music is dedicated to every man,
woman, and child who has found a dream, honors it,
and refuses to let fear talk them out of it.*

*This book was written from the hearts of twelve artists to you.
May you always choose yourself,
and never stop learning the power of your God-given gifts.*

ACKNOWLEDGEMENTS

AFTER WRITING AND RELEASING MUSIC INTO THE WORLD A FEW TIMES, I CAN WHOLE-heartedly say I drastically underestimated the challenge and change of pace involved in writing and releasing a *book*—with *twelve* authors. However, the process has been equally rewarding.

The marriage of music creation and music monetization in this changing industry has been an intense passion for me, and creating this book for our readers is a responsibility I've taken very seriously. Helping artists who have valuable advice to share (at any level of success), and providing that information to acts with a desire to make a living doing what they love, is near and dear to my heart.

The biggest mistake I've made (so far) was not acting on my passion because I was waiting for a sign or a skill I didn't have. But I have gained so much more from life by getting out into the world and *trying* something than I ever did by simply dreaming about it.

Thank you from the bottom of my heart to my incredible mom and brother who never stop believing in me. Dad, I learn more about myself every day from remembering the man you were and the strength I have inside of me. Thank you for that gift. You were here for the conception of this book, and I know you'll be reading it safe in the clouds of heaven.

My deepest gratitude to:

- All the artist and management teams
- JB
- Brodmerkel family
- Dustin
- Taylor, Hannah, Scotty, Brianna, and Lillie
- Brian Moran
- Marla Markman
- TLC Graphics and Narrow Gate Books
- Humphres & Associates
- Fancy

No one would be holding this book without you.

Yours in Music & Success,

Adley Stump

CONTENTS

FOREWORD

EVEN THOUGH WE THOUGHT IT WAS COMPLICATED AT THE TIME, IN HINDSIGHT, IT WAS all so simple then. I'm talking about the path to success in the music business, up until about ten years ago. For decades, there was a fairly common and much pursued route to getting to hit-song, popular-artist status.

First, you had to woodshed and learn your craft in obscurity. Then you got the attention of a manager, who would take you under their wing. You would then build a team that might include an entertainment attorney, a booking agent, a veteran producer, and maybe a publicist.

Once this team was in place, the manager or attorney would shop your songs to A&R reps at various major record labels. If you made it this far, and you were lucky, you might eventually get a record deal and an advance to record your first album.

It was a crap shoot, it was messy, and there was a lot of frustration if you either didn't get signed or got signed but died a slow death in the discount record bin.

Sure, there were exceptions, but this was the primary road to the Music Promised Land.

How times have changed!

Now, more than ever, there is no "common route" to reach an audience and build a career as an artist. Record labels have long lost their luster, and the number of promotional tools at a musician's disposal is staggering. It's confusing, chaotic, and overwhelming.

And I wouldn't want it any other way!

As the many artists profiled in *How They Sell Music* demonstrate, it's an exciting time to be an independent music maker. It's a phenomenal era to play and experiment, and find a path to prominence that works best for you.

In the old-school music biz model, managers and A&R people were the gatekeepers. They were the ones who decided who was worthy of wider exposure. These days, artists and music fans are the new gatekeepers.

It may seem like everyone is recording and releasing music, yet new artists break through all the time—with or without a record label. Now consumers decide what music is worthy of their time, attention, and money.

And, as you will discover in the following pages, the artists who accept this new digital landscape and embrace the workload are enjoying success on their own terms. They are finding creative ways to attract an audience, build meaningful relationships with fans, produce great music, and build their careers.

No matter what you think of the Wild West atmosphere we live in, there will continue to be artists who write and record their own songs, stay focused, cut through the clutter, and end up making a living and making a difference with their music.

Here's an unquestionable fact: There are artists working in relative obscurity right now who will soon rise to prominence a month, six months, or a year from now.

Why couldn't one of those artists be you?

Read the many success stories in *How They Sell Music,* and you just might increase your odds of getting there.

— Bob Baker
Author of the Guerrilla Music Marketing *series of books*
www.TheBuzzFactor.com

INTRODUCTION:
ARE YOU READY TO SELL SOME MUSIC?

IN THIS BOOK, YOU'LL FIND TWELVE STORIES—TWELVE EXAMPLES OF ARTISTS WHO went from *dreaming* of playing music for a living, to actually *doing it*.

Included in these chapters is their advice to help you with your own journey. Every artist has different wisdom to share. Some of the advice will be similar, and some will be conflicting, as no two paths to success are the same. You will need to decide which advice fits your particular situation or which feels the most comfortable to you.

Some of you are just beginning, and others may have fan bases larger than some of the artists in this book. So with that, we don't guarantee that all the advice in every artist's chapter will be helpful to you or provide the information you bought this book looking for. However, we hope that you will find something in every chapter, even if it's only a nugget or two that will be valuable.

We like to think of each of these chapters as mini-books designed to tackle different issues on the path to music industry success. As the artists tell you their story, we hope you will find some tangible takeaways to apply to your own career.

We offer no easy shortcuts or quick tips for attracting a raving fan base and making a living with your art. There are none. We do, however, offer lessons learned the hard way, tips for finding success little by little, how to take those next steps, and the mindset needed to make your dreams a reality.

In the back of the book you'll see that we have compiled a list of incredible tools to help you along the way, and we highly suggest you check them out! You'll find everything from distribution resources and licensing networks to fan acquisition campaigns and social media tools.

We are so happy to be able to bring *How They Sell Music – Volume 1* to you all.

Don't hesitate to reach out to us on all our social media sites with your questions and comments. We are here for ya!

WE HANG OUT HERE

www.HowTheySellMusic.com

Facebook:Facebook.com/HowTheySellMusic

Twitter: @TheySellMusic

Instagram: @HowTheySellMusic

CHAPTER ONE

"The Brand"

BUBBA SPARXXX

Turning Your Biggest "Problem" into Your Golden Opportunity

Ms. New Booty, anyone? Effortlessly and iconically combining country and hip-hop genres, Bubba Sparxxx has created a unique sound that has captured the attention of music lovers for over a decade. He focuses on creating an entire branding experience for his fans and invites them to be a part of a story that is even larger than the music he creates.

WHEN I STARTED IN MUSIC, THERE WAS NO SUCH THING AS COUNTRY RAP. THERE WAS country and there was rap; and my hometown, LaGrange, Georgia, was Country, with a capital C. I was raised hunting and fishing, listening to Waylon Jennings and Willie Nelson.

Then came MTV.

When MTV came on the scene, it was the only place where different kinds of music were available all in one place. I was exposed to a lot of music you wouldn't normally hear in LaGrange. So when I listened to N.W.A. and 2 Live Crew, I heard the spirit of the outlaw music I'd heard all my life.

To me, Dr. Dre and Eazy-E weren't so different from Waylon and Willie. They were just guys creating music, doing what they wanted, and saying what they wanted to say. I may have been raised country, but when it came to music, I fell in love with hip-hop, and because hip-hop is all about being genuine, I knew I could merge backwoods outlaw into my music and it would be a similar vibe. I just combined what I loved with what I knew, and there it was: country rap or "hick-hop." I never thought country music and rap music were too far apart when it came to why people listened to them.

Today, crossover is common and even sought after, but several years ago it was a different story. At first, people didn't know how to react to my style. They didn't know if there was a market, and if so, where it was or how to reach it. Rock stations thought I was too rap and too country. Rap stations wouldn't play my stuff because it was too rock and too country. Country wasn't sure what to do with me at all. Basically, I was too country for everyone but country.

Still, I stayed true to myself and, because hip-hop is built on authenticity, people began to respect that and pay attention. Of course, I got some crazy stares at first and it took a while, but once a few people gave me a chance, more and more people started accepting what I was doing.

But let's go back to the beginning, and I'll walk you through how all this happened.

Go Where the Music Is

Like I said, I was the only white rapper in my little town outside of Atlanta. Because there was no one else like me, and no precedent for white rappers, it never occurred to me that I could make a living rapping. That is, until I got out of LaGrange and involved in the music scenes in the bigger cities in Georgia like Athens and, of course, Atlanta. But I didn't get there on my own.

After high school, my buddy got a football scholarship to the University of Georgia. I wasn't going to college, but I decided it was time to get out of LaGrange, so I moved with him. We had a great time. I would hang out with him in his dorm, and we would stay up late rapping and goofing off.

One night, after a big game, we went back to my buddy's dorm and started doing our thing. People started gathering around, and my buddy started telling people that I was a rapper signed with So So Def Records.

I wasn't, obviously, but we thought it would impress the ladies (as if he being a football player wasn't enough). Turns out, the ladies weren't the only ones paying attention.

Later that night, one of the guys who had been hanging around listening came up and introduced himself and started talking about the music industry. His name was Bobby Stamps, and it turned out he knew people at So So Def!

At first, I thought he was just joking around, but when I figured out he was the real deal, I pulled him aside to explain that we were just being dumb and trying to impress girls. Lucky for me, Bobby liked my stuff. He believed in me, saw my talent and desire, and started introducing me to the people he knew in the industry. He's been my manager ever since!

Through Bobby and other connections, I got involved in the Athens and Atlanta music scenes. I would get together with other artists, and we'd just rap with each other and share our stuff. We'd go back and forth, established musicians and newbies like me, doing what we love. When I realized that I could hold my own in such talented company, that's when I started believing that I could actually make a living in music.

Find an "In"

Meeting Bobby was huge for me, not just because he's been a great friend and manager, but also because he was able to set up meetings through his connections. With Bobby by my side working the business end, I was able to focus on what I truly love—the music. I know it's a cliché, but it's true: It's not what you know, but who you know, that matters. Connections are so important. You need to meet people who can help you make a personal contact.

You want someone to be your manager? You need an agent? You want to book a gig? Find a contact; find an "in." Maybe you're great at talking yourself up, maybe you're not. Honestly, that doesn't always matter. I can talk myself up all day long. But if I can get *someone else* to talk me up, now that has some impact.

It looks cooler to have other people talking about you than *you* talking about you. If you're in a room with a music influencer or someone you want to know about you, try having someone *else* talk to them first and bring you up in conversation, say what a bad ass you are, and offer to make the introduction.

But don't expect them to jump on board with you right away. If they're legit, they're busy, and they want to watch what you're doing on your own first. They don't want someone who just wants to be told what to do and will expect the manager to do the heavy-lifting—especially since a manager's pay is typically around 10 percent of gross profits.

There has to be something already existing—and great—or at least very close to existing for them to make money with.

Build the relationship naturally and let them build confidence in you. Get them wanting *you*—not you wanting them. Whoever cares the least controls the relationship.

Set the Right Tone

If you take the plunge and move to a city like Nashville or Atlanta, it's pretty easy to spot who's new to town. They're the ones talking about "everything they have going on." The ones who actually do have stuff going on don't talk about it unless they're asked. They don't flaunt it. They don't need to.

If you move to one of these cities where there is more accessible opportunity (out of sight, out of mind!), you have to carry yourself with a calm confidence, and you have to stand out without trying to stand out. You can always spot the guy or girl across the room who is trying to act cool or is out of his or her element... you don't want to be *that* person!

You only get a first impression once, and you don't want to set your precedence in town as the super-naïve one or someone who tried to take meetings with the bigwigs before you were truly ready.

Don't seek meetings with labels, management, or booking agencies until you are confident enough to say that if this was your one shot, you would be fine with it. If you would be at your complete best in seven months, it's better to wait seven months. I promise, trying to take the big meetings too early will hurt you way more than help you, and you will look back wishing you had waited.

Big meetings will come from someone who knows industry insiders and who is comfortable enough to put their name on the line and vouch for you. But it is also you who is attaching your name to that person. How well do you really know them and their reputation? If you only get one shot at this meeting, is *this* the person you want waving your flag and representing your brand?

Don't settle for taking the quick route; it won't serve you well. Take the time to get to know the people you surround yourself with and build your relationships over time.

If you are a songwriter, a good start is getting a meeting with BMI, ASCAP, SESAC, or another performing rights organization (PRO). Pick the PRO that you have a good relationship with and sense that they get you. They can open a lot of doors when you are ready.

Find the Right Path

Many artists are breaking in by first being a songwriter. Just because that's happening more and more, though, doesn't mean it's right for you. You've got to figure out if that's the path you want to walk. Because if it is, it's a long road of getting cuts, getting into the right writing circles, and then proving your talent once you're in them. It's also based on someone believing that your songs are incredible and getting them to the right people.

If you're just a songwriter looking for cuts, look at some of the licensing resources we've provided and get feedback on your songs to see if they really have what it takes to compete commercially. If you're a writer and can sing, sing your own songs, and create a story around what you do, put content out consistently, and make it interesting for people to be involved. You can create a video series leading up to your single release, pair your album with a charity to donate a percentage of the profits, and get some good public relations. Do a blog post each week about the story behind the music or why you wrote it. Give something to your audience for them to relate to and make them feel something that's worth telling their friends about.

Again, there is no formula or guarantee of what will work. But doing work and putting yourself out there is the only way to get anywhere. Nothing grows in shadows.

Get Outside Your Bubble

The best thing you can do when you move to a new city is get a good group of friends around you in the industry. Careful, though: You want to attract them, not desperately try to find them. Form an informal "advisory board" of friends whom you can bounce ideas off and grow with.

Many times, people move to town thinking they are going to be best friends with the established hit makers. That surely they will see how awesome you are and welcome you kindly into their group. You may hit a streak of luck, but my best general advice is you've got to understand they already have their groups. They came up together, failed together, and found success together. Until you get to town and experience that, it's hard to understand. You've got to find your own group that will ride or die with you, and you hustle together and be the next wave of something new, instead of trying to get in with people who have been best friends for years.

It takes a while to figure out each city's dynamics and the way it works—a couple years I would say for sure to really get it. That's why it's important to be present and build your relationships over time.

A Stand-Out Name

One way I was able to be unique when I got to the bigger cities was to come up with a new, flavorful name people would remember. Once again, I wanted to find something that symbolized both my country roots and my hip-hop style. Believe it or not, I was the runt of my family, so everyone called me "Lil' Bubba," or just Bubba, for short. I knew Bubba summed up what I wanted to represent cultur-ally, so that part was easy. The last name was a little harder.

Bobby introduced me to a producer he thought would get me, named Shannon Houchins. Shannon and I got together to think up names, and the Rodney Dangerfield movie *Wally Sparks* was lying there. Shannon said, "What about Bubba Sparks?" and we knew in-stantly that we'd found it. To add some flavor, I changed the "ks" to "xxx"—and Bubba Sparxxx was born.

Find Your Champion

From there, in a roundabout way, someone else taking action on my behalf ended up opening the door to my biggest break. With the name figured out, Shannon and I started recording and trying to get my music out there. Shannon sent my music to Doug Kaye at New-town Music Group in Sarasota, Florida. Doug liked what he heard and said if we could get him a completed album, he'd distribute it. He didn't offer to promote the album or do any marketing, but it turns out, down the line, he was the one who first got me on the track to signing with Interscope Records.

If you can get a champion in your corner who will push for you, espe-cially one with connections and a good reputation, then his contacts will typically trust him and the acts he's invested in. You can get to know contacts on LinkedIn and Music Xray, Twitter, or create an alias acting as your manager, or have someone you trust send a profes-sional email to a company you're interested in to request a meeting. And then make sure you are ready: Have a product that shows who you are and what you represent; know where you want to go; and be clear what you are asking for once you make the connection.

We knew what we were asking for. Right after I put out that independ-ent release, Doug found out Fred Durst, from Limp Bizkit, was going to be at a specific studio at a specific date and time. So he decided to wrap up my CD and drop it in the mail to Westlake Recording Studios in Los Angeles, "ATTN: Fred Durst." We asked him to listen it, because we thought I would be a good fit for Interscope, where Fred was VP at the time. It was wild! Personally, I don't think it's a great idea to just randomly spam unsolicited music to industry people. I've never heard of anyone making it big in the industry just by tweeting or cold-calling the powers that be. You have to make that personal connection. Emails are a dime a dozen, but if you can make the effort to get face time, it shows you are that much more serious.

So believe it or not (I couldn't), Fred got my CD, listened to it, and called me up himself. We talked about a record deal. We made a lot of plans—a lot of promises—but it all fell through in the end. It wasn't that Fred was full of it; he and I are good friends now. Now that I've put in some time, I have a better understanding of the industry, and I know it was just one of those things that wasn't meant to be.

I could have let that setback stop me dead in my tracks. I wanted to be at Interscope so bad and was so close, I could taste it! But I knew I couldn't let that blow stop me; I knew I just had to work that much harder.

Never. Give. Up.

People tell me all the time that they dream of having a career in music, but, really, that's all it is, a dream. They want to play or write or sing or rap, but they don't want to put in the time, work, and sacrifices to make it happen. They just want to be discovered and have someone else develop them on their dime. If people took all the energy and time they spent looking for shortcuts and tricks for easy success, and actually spent it on working to earn it, there would be a lot more success stories.

If you want something bad enough, you have to hustle every day like someone is trying to take it from you. There are artists who are willing to put in the work and investment in themselves, and if you look at the ones who have made it, nine times out of ten, they outlasted and outworked everyone else creatively.

Getting to that point though where you have other people who believe in you, and especially a manager and a lawyer to guide the business end for you, can make all the difference in getting your music out there. There are going to be days when you want to give up and when your faith is weak. At those times, knowing someone else believes in you and is there for you will give you the strength to keep going. Get that good group around you—friends in the industry who get it and can cheer you on.

You can't live each day being miserable, just waiting to be happy once you get that object of your desire. What if you never get it? You want to focus on your strengths and what you're good at and work those because that's what makes the journey enjoyable.

On the flip side, you can think and believe you really have what it takes, but that isn't going to get you anywhere without massive action and ingenuity. If I had a dollar for every time someone said, "Man, you blew up overnight!" I wouldn't have to work another day in my life. There is no such thing as an overnight success. Believing that "Point A" is making music in my mom's basement and "Point B" is getting a Grammy—that's just not reality. That's more like A and Z—you still have to go through all the other letters in between. And all those letters in between are the tough ones. That's where you'll make leaps and bounds. But it's also where you'll make mistakes. It's where you discover how bad you really want this.

That glamorous lifestyle is so tempting, but it's not reality. It's an illusion. But don't let that get you down. Stay in the game. You *will* go through low points, and once you're down, it's very difficult to get back up. If you slip up, remember that everyone makes mistakes, so don't beat yourself up. Set up a plan and a strategy, and don't look back at what you could have done differently. That won't do anything to help you.

When they sent that CD to Fred, I was definitely at a low point. I was so broke; if the power in my apartment wasn't cut off, it was something else. I couldn't afford to put gas in my '78 Ford Courier, but I couldn't afford to lose faith either. I kept faith in God and my talent, and I kept going. I continued to believe in my ability to make music and make a living out of it. People saw that I wasn't giving up and, because of that, they continued to believe in me too.

Even when my first big letdown happened with Fred, I didn't give up on myself and I didn't give up on Interscope. I had gotten my hopes up, and even though I was still in a bad place financially, I wasn't going to let a little setback get me down. I was more determined than ever. One day at a time, for about a year, I got up and did what I had to do to find another "in" at Interscope.

An Unlikely "In"

I just knew that's where I wanted to be, and I was bound and determined. Around that time, Shannon and Doug, my distributor, teamed up to form the production company 11th Hour Entertainment and signed me on. Again, Shannon reached out to connections and gave my music to Eric Williams, a friend of his who worked in administration at Interscope. Eric had already heard my music and become a fan because Fred had circulated the project through the office.

Eventually, they found another believer who would not be denied. In the end, it wasn't a corporate guy who brought me in, it was a guy named Gerardo—you might remember him as "Rico Suave." Gerardo got me in the door at Interscope through Eric's relationship with him, signed me on, and took me under his wing. I always credit Gerardo as *the* guy who made things happen for me at Interscope. He took a big chance on me and my new take on music—especially knowing the resistance we had mixing genres. Having him behind me was a huge deal, and I'm so blessed to have had him believe in and champion me.

What's Your "Something More"?

Even then, it wasn't easy. It shouldn't be. I told you how hard it was for me to get radio play at first. But now that's not your only outlet to get heard. Today, anyone can record and post songs online. YouTube, Facebook, Twitter...there are endless possibilities. To be honest, that's both an opportunity and an obstacle. Sure, you can post your music anywhere, but so can everyone else. You need to do something to set yourself apart. Why would people listen to *your* stuff over someone else's? Not just because it's "better." How are you branding yourself differently and getting the word out there?

You've got to be first, better, or different. What's your "something more"?

My "something more" was mixing genres. At the time, it felt more like a challenge than a bonus. I didn't fit in. There was nothing even resembling a road map or formula to follow. We had to make it up as we went along. I could have said, "This isn't working. No one gets me. It's too difficult. I'm too different. I give up." Or I could have conformed to what was already working. But that wouldn't have gotten me anywhere. I got where I am because I was different and I stood out. I wasn't doing what was working at the time.

Look at your music. What gives you the most problems? What makes you "different"? That might just be your opportunity! Don't fight it—use it!

This is a lot of what I did to take initiative before I had a great team around me on the label. Because once I got there, it was a whole different level of opportunity. Talking about creating value, and what that means and looks like is easy, but how do you do it? I imagine this is where most of you are at in your careers, and it is certainly the most important time.

PRO TIPS

GET YOUR MUSIC HEARD

- *Find an "in."* Making connections in the music industry allows you to get your foot in the door. When you have others who are on board and in support with what you are doing, you will look even more credible and be able to gain more attention when your voice isn't the only thing vouching for you.

- *Make friends in the industry.* When you have a group of like-minded individuals in the same industry you are trying to succeed in, you are given the support you need, along with vicarious experience that will benefit you. Plus, your exposure will increase as you consistently have people backing you up.

- *Stand out without trying to.* You need to find a way to be unique in this industry, but you never want to push it. Key in to what makes you stand out and work with that, but don't try to make something work if it wouldn't naturally.

After I signed with Interscope, Dr. Dre introduced the world to another white rapper: Marshall Mathers (aka Eminem). With Dr. Dre behind him, Eminem exploded onto the scene. The attention he generated helped bring awareness to what I was doing, too, because now there was a market for white rappers and it resonated with people because it was so honest. It was a huge blessing because it opened airplay avenues for music like mine and gave even more substance to the work of white rappers—even a country one. It's still a sort of "alt" genre without a place to truly fit in on radio.

Boom—Chemistry!

Let's get back to Gerardo and how he helped me. He set me up with a few different producers but struggled to find that specific chemistry to make my next record. Then producer and co-founder of Interscope, Jimmy Iovine, played my music to producer and rapper Timbaland—and *boom!*—chemistry. He loved it. Timbaland worked on the rerelease of my debut album, "Dark Days, Bright Nights," including my first and No. 1 single "Ugly." He also helped me evolve to the next level. With his help, my songs matured to telling the deeper stories of the countryside, similar to what traditional rappers did with the "streets." From working-class people busting their butts to barely make ends meet to the drug epidemic plaguing small towns, there was so much more of the story to tell, and a new way to tell it. Focusing on these stories, I wrote some of the best lyrics of my life.

It wasn't just my lyrics that matured. Timbaland drew out more from the deep country style, incorporating bluegrass, blues, and rock into the instrumentation. He sampled bluegrass and honky-tonk albums and brought in exceptional musicians to add country flavor with fiddles, violins, harmonica, horns, and guitar. The result was my critically acclaimed sophomore album, "Deliverance."

At first, the label resisted "Deliverance" because it didn't fit into the neat little urban radio package set by my first album, especially "Ugly." It was a huge gamble at the time, but the label came around and accepted the challenge. We believed the fresh sound in "Deliverance" could transcend the obstacles, and it did—it just took eight years!

Expand Your Audience with Collaboration

Personally, I love a challenge. My latest challenge has been trying to participate and engage in the Nashville songwriting community. The most important aspect for me, as a hip-hop artist, is crafting genuine lyrics. It's such a personal process that it's easy to get stuck in that introverted place. That's so different from the Nashville mentality. In Nashville, people work together and write for each other. That's been a huge challenge for me. Sitting in a room with other people who want to help me write my lyrics...that's just not how hip-hop works. It's a credibility thing. I have to write my own stuff. It has to come from me. But that doesn't mean I can't still learn from other people and collaborate on the choruses and be exposed to crafting music in a way I couldn't have done on my own.

If you're uncomfortable writing in a room with other people, do it. If you're intimidated by solitude, find a quiet place and settle in. You'll learn something at the very least! You don't have to turn your process upside down or do anything untrue to who you are, but you should always be open to growing, becoming the best you can be, and then becoming even better. It may make you uneasy, but who knows, that little bit of squirming might just move you to a new and improved place and build some cool new relationships.

Getting advice or bouncing ideas off of someone is not selling out; it's smart. We don't normally change on our own. We need help. Change and growth take outside influence, recommendations, and insight. It takes working with others—something we aren't always willing to do. Truth is, working with others not only helps you improve, but it can also be a great way to extend your market *and* your network.

Collaborating is one of the best ways to push myself and expand my audience. A big part of hip-hop is sampling other artists and songs, playing off each other and integrating genres. It's a form of respect and a nod to our influences. Throughout my career, I've been blessed to not only sample, but to collaborate with artists I look up to, like Timbaland, Archie Eversole, the Ying Yang Twins, Colt Ford, and Danny Boone from Rehab, not to mention people behind the scenes like Jimmy Iovine and production crew Organized Noize. Each time I work with someone, I walk away with something new, just like when I was first starting out and rapping with people in Atlanta. Working with other artists inspires me and pushes me to keep growing and evolving.

Social Media Is Mandatory

Post photos on social media sites from your latest writing and collaboration sessions. Tag your collaborators and provide links to their sites (just make sure to have the links open in a new tab or window; you don't want to direct people away from your site completely). Be who you are, and don't hide from it. And if you work with others, give credit where credit is due.

Speaking of social media, it is an excellent tool to show your true self and let people in on the inner workings of the artists and music they love. Use Instagram, Snapchat, Vine, and Twitter; people love the intimacy of seeing what you're doing *right now*. People want to feel a part of your life. So use these tools to your advantage to create something worth watching, not just posting what you're eating for lunch. That's not going to grow your brand and create a community that people are so proud to be a part of.

The MTV generation got to see all kinds of music mixed together, be exposed to new music, and have their horizons broadened in a way the industry had never done before. Social media, however, has helped bring artists back to their own unique identities and is a *must* to compete in the market today. If you don't know how to do it or don't want to, find someone to help you. But understand that the personal touch of social media is what people crave, so it really is best to take care of most of it yourself and not just have someone do it for you.

I like to post pictures hanging with my friends and just being a goof. That reinforces what they already know about me through my lyrics and gives them an inside look at the source. We can't just use social media to post about our shows. That information is good, but it's also listed other places. Let people see *you*. Being real with my fans has done nothing but make my artistry stronger.

When it comes down to it, people want to relate. For me, that's talking to people who love rap and country. I didn't know there was an audience for that until I realized that I was the audience. My friends were the audience. They listened to country and lived in the country, but listened to and related to rap. So I related to them in return and created my music for them. But the process of having a successful career and getting it to the masses came with "perfect storm" timing, when record labels held the golden key. Now, they don't. The fans do.

Creating a Fan Base

How can *you* build an amazing following? How can *you* get raving fans? There isn't one answer. You could try to copy what I did or what other people have done, and it still won't happen the same way. There's social media as I just said, but nothing can compare to the power of a live show and meeting fans face to face. The easy access of social media and online entertainment can be a great tool, but it can also be just as easily ignored. Online audiences are not necessarily captive audiences. They're listening to music, watching TV, flipping through social media, hopping from one website to the next. You have to know exactly who you are marketing to and where they are hanging out looking for content to absorb.

Are they on blogs? Forums? Do they play video games, or do they play on tractors and hay bales? You have to know who your audience is, because it's not going to be everyone, as much as you'd like to think it will be. You're better to target a smaller group and have them be insanely loyal than a huge market that's half enthusiastic about you.

At a live show, people are much more likely to pay attention and get into what you're doing when they've paid to get into it and have nowhere else to go. They don't even have to be there to see you. Opening for other bands is one of the best ways to build an audience of your own. *To get people in front of you, you have to find a way to get in front of them.* And when you get that opportunity to play for people, make sure you are something to talk about and are memorable. What can you incorporate into your show that they have never seen before? Build your tribe one fan at a time. Remember, "what's your something more"?

As a bonus, opening for people helped me make connections with more and more people in the industry, which meant my name and music spread further. Eventually, I was setting up my own headlining gigs and, in time, hitting the road for shows myself. By opening for groups who came to my town, I not only got to piggyback off of their success and reach more people in my area, but I also got the opportunity to meet people who could set me up with their connections and audience base in their hometowns. It's a long process, and not easy, but if you want a music career, this is what it takes.

I started by checking out the local scene: music venues, coffee shops, bars, open mics, concert series, writers' nights, anywhere I might be able to get my music heard. I went to shows. I got to know the people who worked at the venues, especially the people who took care of booking. I didn't try to become best friends with everyone, but it helps to get on the radar. Again I made sure to be genuine about it. People know when you're just there for yourself, trying to make connections. If that's true, don't pretend it's not. Let them know you'd love to meet who's in charge and talk about booking a show. Then buy the guy a drink. Honestly, I learned the smart thing to do in these situations is to use any and every experience as an opportunity to learn the ropes, not just to promote myself.

Once you've got those live shows booked, take the opportunity to extend your reach. Live stream it, tweet it, post it, or ask for retweets or for whatever you want. If someone hits you up on Twitter, return the favor. I'm telling you right now, if you open for me or are at one of my shows, get on Twitter and give me some love: "Great show tonight with Bubba Sparxxx! @TheRealBubbaK @Venue." You can bet I'll pass along the love.

Another way I get the audience involved is taking pictures of the crowd from the stage and then posting them to social media during the show, right there from the stage. I tell them I'm posting a picture and encourage the crowd to tag themselves, reply, and repost. That gets their attention, draws them in, and makes them an active part of the show, as well as creating a personal moment with them. Even if it wasn't my audience in the beginning, if I was opening, I've found that if I engage them, they will be mine by the end of the show.

Challenge Accepted

I strongly believe all the challenges we face pursuing a music career, especially in the earlier stages, make us stronger and are so important to either our failure or our success. They grow us as an artist. They give us reasons to write and a story to tell.

There will be so many challenges that are out of your control (like media coverage and genre acceptance), but there are also challenges you can step into willingly to improve your music and yourself.

I always say, "Either you're getting better, or you're getting worse." Focus on getting better, doing at least one thing every day that gets you closer to your goals. You'll be surprised how far you can get in just 365 days.

Thanks for reading, and I hope you keep at it! The only person who can keep you down is *you*!

Peace,

Bubba Sparxxx

CHAPTER TWO

"The Go-Getters"

CIMORELLI

How to Build a Career in Your Teens—with Wisdom, Honesty, and Humility

Six sisters with undeniable talent kick-started their career by posting a video to YouTube that went viral overnight. Full of wisdom and humility, these girls are the perfect example of building a career in your early teens, creating a strong team, and formulating a brand that has resonated with young girls around the world. Signed to Universal Records, these young ladies continue to shoulder most of the work themselves and exemplify what it means to be strong and honest women in the face of imminent fame.

WE'RE CHRISTINA, KATHERINE, LISA, AMY, LAUREN, AND DANI—AND TOGETHER we're Cimorelli.

Before we dive deeper into what we do, how we started, and how we got to where we are today, here's a little tidbit about each of us so you have us straight in your minds: Christina is the eldest, at 24, and the leader of the group. Katherine's next at 22; she's the writer of the family. Following closely is Lisa, who's 21 and a bit of a perfectionist. Amy's 19 and a self-proclaimed social butterfly. Lauren is 16 and quite possibly the most laid-back person in the world, while Dani, at 14, is loud and vivacious—the exact opposite.

With introductions out of the way, let's get down to business.

Small-Town Roots and Dreams

Our first exposure to music started when we were all in the womb. Our mom's a classical pianist, and we're convinced that we've heard her practicing and playing the piano from day one. We were born with it—it's in our blood!

Our mom taught us all how to sing when we were really young—between the ages of 2 and 4. She went all out: getting us into the church choir, teaching us about harmonies through singing barbershop and vocal jazz. All of us were pretty into it, and given the fact that our mom was a music major and a choir director for musical theater and church choir, we'd go as far as to say that singing came naturally to us. We've all grown up on a steady diet of classical music and the '80s greatest hits.

Initially, when our mom suggested we officially form a band, we kind of shot her down. After a couple of years, some of us changed our minds, but it was a little difficult to actually wrangle all of us out of our other activities to focus on just one thing.

The eldest three, namely Katherine, Lisa, and Christina, began performing locally in 2002, doing barbershop and vocal jazz in and around our town. A few years down the line, Amy and Lauren joined us, too, with Dani joining later.

Back then, we were just the Cimorelli girls, who liked to sing a little bit. In our small town outside Sacramento, California, we were very involved in theater, drama, and music individually, but we didn't stand out—not like some kids do—as people who are destined to make it big.

You Have to Start Somewhere

We became Cimorelli, "the band," with the five of us—excluding Dani because she was really young—officially in 2007. Our oldest brother, Mike, played guitar for us, and we would tour in random, small places and do various shows and events—anywhere we'd be lucky enough to get booked. We even sang these really old classical songs, a cappella, at different nursing homes—gigs our grandma would help us get. We did a whole lot of things during that time, but nothing really stuck or made much of an impact.

In the initial couple of years after the band's formation, we were all just playing instruments and singing and making music, promoting ourselves, and trying to build a fan base somehow, but it didn't really seem to work. We even released an EP of some of the songs we wrote and recorded ourselves. That wasn't much of a success either.

If It Worked for Miley...

In 2009 we saw a leaked performance of Miley Cyrus' song "Party in the USA" on a gossip website about young celebrities. Given the scandal and controversy that surrounded the leak of this song, Katherine suggested that we record a cover of it and put it up on

YouTube, because we knew people would probably be searching for the leaked video and maybe they would find ours. While we were all familiar with YouTube, even sometimes posting our own original songs and performances on our channel, we hadn't really thought about that type of strategy before, and while initially we were a little skeptical and hesitant, we forged ahead with the plan.

From time to time, the gossip website featured covers of the most popular songs, so Lisa took a shot and emailed our version of it to them. Lo and behold, our cover got featured!

We didn't really expect anything to come of it because we already had a YouTube channel and we were posting videos to it sporadically, but, at most, we'd only ever received a couple of hundred views. Imagine our surprise when we woke up the next morning, after being featured, and we saw that our little cover had been viewed over 20,000 times! Saying that we all went a little mental, shrieking and screaming in excitement, would be an understatement.

Continuing the Momentum

After a full day to digest the fact that we were being watched by so many people, we decided that we absolutely had to follow up on this. This couldn't be a one-off thing, especially not when we were trying so hard to build some semblance of a fan base and not getting anywhere.

The next week we put together and posted another cover song, this time of an original Disney song called "Send It On". Full of harmonies and an a cappella cover, when it went live on our YouTube channel, it got a good number of views, too, because that first cover got us several hundred subscribers who were automatically notified of our new video.

That's when the light bulb went on—when we realized "Hey, we're onto something here, and people actually like us!" Those YouTube covers were what catapulted us into an insane whirlwind of comments and social media. We decided that we should continue with the cover videos, be consistent with them, and just try our best to improve with each one.

Take the Good with the Bad

With all that publicity, though, you get *a lot* of hate comments and reviews. At first, it stung really badly, but then we realized it's just not healthy to dwell on it.

When the "Party in the USA" cover blew up, we started getting all sorts of these messages and comments, and we were so excited about it. We *never* had any messages in the past couple years of posting original content, so this was a big change. What's more, we started to welcome the hate messages, because that's what proved that people cared and were at least watching.

If this is an industry you desire to be in, you *can't* let the hate and the negativity bring you down. Someone told us once that the people with the negative opinions are almost always the ones who speak up the most, and the ones with a more positive outlook are those who actually go out and buy your music. They don't always take the time to leave comments.

It Only Takes One

Among those hundreds of comments and messages that we received on our cover videos, there was one that really stood out. We'd managed to capture the attention of a 13-year-old girl, who was all the way in the United Kingdom. She said her mom was a big music manager and she was interested in talking to us.

Lisa saw it, and in her excitement and eagerness, didn't stop to think it through before replying back and just giving this girl our mom's number! The next thing we know, Sarah Stennett's calling our mother and telling her how interested she is in managing us! Thank God she turned out to be a real manager and not a crazy person!

Signer Beware

While we were lucky that Sarah was truly a legitimate individual working in the music industry, albeit on another continent, we know there are so many others who have not been so fortunate.

This mystical idea of a manager, an agent, a music label, and a recording deal can be overwhelming and difficult to wrap your mind around—trust me, we all understand that because we were the same way—but you cannot let that affect your judgment. For people trying to break into the music industry—basically people like us, who didn't grown up in such an environment or haven't been exposed to all the glamour that comes along with being in the limelight—this shiny industry can be really mystifying. The idea of a manager or agent wanting you seems so crazy and exciting, but there are a lot of sharks out there just waiting to pounce and grab onto the opportunity that your talent may present. The music industry seems like a magical world that most people don't live in or even get to see inside; however, like every magical kingdom, there is always a dark side, and you have to try and steer clear of it and keep good guidance around you.

You have to be diligent and careful when you take a chance on someone and put your life and reputation in their hands. It's a very scary thought: signing your life and talent away to someone else. They could be truly successful in the world but not morally sound. When someone offers to partner with you, as hard as it is, do your due diligence to see if they are legit and "get" you.

People go to great lengths to gain a new artist's trust and build credibility with them just to get them to sign and take their money. You really need to be aware of what's going on in your surroundings, and keep your eyes and ears wide open. Unless you've done your research, don't blindly trust anyone. Don't just jump at the first person who seems interested in representing you. This is your life and blood we're talking about, your hard work and talent. It's a gamble and a risk, and you eventually have to go with *someone* if you want to breakthrough in the music industry, but remember, be cautious and smart and never hurt anyone. Plus, it will show them you are smart and not a desperate artist who's willing to jump in with just anyone.

Next Stop: LA and a Recording Contract

Sarah contacted our mom, and a week later she had one of her associates fly in from LA to visit us. We put on a good show: We played some of our original songs from our very first EP and introduced them to our music and style.

I guess you could say that things worked out really well for us. Sarah really liked our music and personalities, and for the next few years, she was our manager. The funniest thing, though, was at that point, we had never even been to LA or branched out from our little hometown. Strange how these things go; when you really don't expect much, everything seems to fall into place all by itself.

Sarah was the one who brought us to LA for the first time. We now had management and representation, and with Sarah's help, we were taking meetings and looking for a record label to sign with. Since Sarah had all the connections we needed at the time, we frequently traveled to LA and met people from multiple record labels.

While most of them liked us, none of them were really sure what to do with us. We were six wholesome sisters, but everyone tried to make us more edgy. They liked us a lot, but when you are going to put a ton of money behind someone, there has to be strategic positioning, and it was hard for everyone to find the balance. That's when we met with the people from Universal Music UK. At that point, we'd already met a bunch of different people who we didn't really connect with, however, Universal Music was like a breath of fresh air.

Given Sarah's expertise in these matters, she thought this label was most passionate about our music and us, and she advised us this was the right way to go. So we signed a record deal with Universal Music UK in 2010.

Playing on Wholesome

What was it that appealed to these big-shot music industry individuals? I think there are two things that really worked in our favor. One, our wholesome family-oriented image, and two, the fact that we already had somewhat of a fan base and following on social media.

That's not to say we had billions of fans and everyone was screaming our name everywhere we went—no. But we had a good amount of people who were following us on YouTube, and they were the ones who actually waited for our videos to come out and interacted with us.

To get signed to a label, you need to figure out your assets and play on them. When we started, we built on and projected the things we were best at: a cappella singing and harmonies, with a little twist on instruments thrown in for good measure. We combined that with something else that made us stand out in the crowd: our family values and love for each other. Sounds corny, doesn't it? It does to us, too, but that's the truth.

Record labels were interested in us because we represented all the things you don't regularly see in the music business. Some of the past family acts—the Jackson 5, Hanson, the Jonas Brothers—were big and so successful because they brought something unique to the table. It wasn't just some random bunch of people who were put together. Of course, that's not to say that doesn't work—look at One Direction. But these groups have an *image*, and it is consistent across *everything* they do. *And* it appeals to the biggest music-buying audience: teen and pre-teen girls.

Your brand doesn't have to appeal to everyone, though (and that's not even possible). Often you get the strongest fan base by purposely not tailoring to people who don't subscribe to your mentality. It makes the bond you have with your followers even deeper because you think and feel the same way about certain things, and it's a bonding element. That comes naturally when you stick up for something that may be unpopular, but it's what you believe and what is true to you. Whether it's your values, or your political party, or the kind of music you listen to, be strong in what you stand for, and it will attract the most devoted followers.

We filled that void for a family-oriented act, and that appealed to the label because there wasn't much like us out there. When you are trying to gain the attention of record labels, focus on the points that make you different from the rest of the acts on the market and different than anything else they have on their roster.

When you try and become "the next Katy Perry," instead of being inspired by her and putting your own spin on it, you aren't going to be called the new Katy Perry. No one will take her place; she already has her neighborhood built.

Instead, you'll just be known as the person who's trying to copy Katy Perry and be the not-so-good version of her. You can borrow ideas and things you like that others have done, but it never ever works in an artist's favor to directly copy a sound or style. People can see that it's not genuine or unique.

For example, if you're going to go the YouTube cover route, like us, you can just do a plain cover of the song where you're kind of imitating another artist's sound, or you can completely change it and put your own spin on it. Imitating another artist may be OK for the first couple videos, when you're trying to find your footing, but bringing your own sound to a song and making it different is a much better path to follow. We've got the a capella and harmonies bit going for us, where we change the songs and make them our own. You can try something like that or even take inspiration from countless other successful YouTube artists. Consider Karmin—the dynamic duo of Amy Heidemann and Nick Noonan. They started on YouTube and completely went viral when Amy rapped this insanely cool version of Chris Brown's "Look at Me Now"—and nailed it! No one had seen anything like it, and it spread like wildfire!

Build a Following—Get Signed (Not the Other Way Around)

We know of bands that have gotten signed on the spot because of their musical abilities but have no following—and you know what's the first thing that they've been told by their labels after scrawling pretty little signatures on the dotted lines? Build a social media personality and get a fan following. Labels are way more likely to sign you if you have built your following on your own and show you care enough about your career to do so. They don't have the development budgets like they used to.

The labels or management used to help you find your sound and image and help you craft it step by step. But that's becoming extremely rare. There are still instances when someone will be ushered into a record deal quickly, even if they're completely off the grid, and everything will be done for them so the labels can make a quick buck, but that's very rare.

Record labels have realized that artists can build their fan following themselves, so now they're giving precedence to those who already seem to be a little known and have wanted it bad enough to do the legwork. It really just makes their jobs easier and ours that much harder.

Doing all the grunt work yourself and building artistic credibility on a social media platform yourself is actually a good thing because if a label invests into your development, it's an advance, and you have to pay back every dime of it. If you get a tour bus, it goes into your debt against the label. If someone from the label goes out to lunch with someone and talks about you, the label pays for that, and it *also* gets added to your debt.

Think of it like this: With a good understanding of how to use the Internet to your advantage, plus your fabulous music, relatable content, and your attractive brand, you have the power in your hands. The more famous you are on any social media platform, the more leverage you have to negotiate a record deal on your terms. You can go, "Hey, people like this, like me, what I do, and how I do it, and that's something that can be beneficial for the both of us." Just be nice about it, and you'll have the ball in your court. You've got to build a business that another business (label, publisher, manager) wants to acquire.

Signing Is the Start—Not the End—of the Work

When we got signed, we were so excited. We thought this is where it all ends. It's like the climax point of a movie—we've got it made now that we have a record deal. We were thinking, "Where's the Grammy stage?! We've been signed!" We failed to realize that was the point where the hard work really started. But at least we had a team!

Contrary to our beliefs, which had us looking for magical stepping-stones all laid out for us, we still had to do so much on our own. When you have a record company take you on as an artist, keep in mind you are not the only one. A record company may have hundreds of other acts they're managing and overseeing.

PRO TIPS

GET YOUR YOUTUBE VIDEO SEEN

- *Have a plan.* You can't just put up a YouTube video every once in a while and expect it to do well—unless you have a large promotional budget or you have built an audience. The algorithm for exposure is based off consistency and great content. If you don't work to accomplish both, you will only have mediocre viewership.

- *Find an alternative distribution system.* If you're hosting your video on YouTube, how can you drive traffic to it outside of YouTube? How about a magazine write-up? Or does the video pertain to the interests of a group you can partner with for it's release, and they can help you drive traffic. Think of creative ways to distribute the content and drive traffic with each new release.

- *Tag your YouTube content appropriately.* We learned that the most frequent tags people use on YouTube, or any network, when looking for new music, are general tags, like "happy song," "sad song," or "fun song." Use those, then add in the details of the song itself. Collectively, that will raise your chances of coming up faster in social media searches.

You have to find a way to grab and keep their attention by continuing to do the same work you were doing that got you signed in the first place. They have a certain amount of money they can spend, but they aren't going to be placing any bets on you if they're even a little bit unsure of how profitable you will be to the company. You've got to let them know that you're worth the effort.

A thought that rarely crosses any artist's mind is just how much pressure the record label people are under. If they take a chance on you and push you through, and you fail to garner the response they're hoping for, they could lose their jobs and that would possibly mean the end of their career, and subsequently, yours as well. If you can lessen their risk, you'll have the best chance of the label being a great platform instead of a hindrance.

Just as you're hesitant to put your faith in someone, they are too. Sometimes record labels might not even push you through at all just because of this uncertainty that surrounds you as an artist. We've discovered that you have to be willing to work hard to prove yourself, even after you're signed, to show them you will work even harder than they will and that you aren't expecting all the work and creativity to be handled by them.

We've been signed for a few years now, and we still do most of the work ourselves. We will divide our parts in songs, compose music, harmonize melodies, brainstorm our videos, and even record them ourselves. Lisa spends hours at a time editing our cover videos before posting them on our YouTube channel.

Don't think of a record deal as the top step of a ladder. We compare a record label to the engine of the car, maybe the driving force, but it's not the entire car. The label acts like a bank and has the *relationships* to promote you as they see fit. You are a product they market and sell. But to get the promotion you want, you've got to continually show them you have a product that is ready and willing to do all the hard work it takes.

Fan-Base Building 101

It's safe to say we've concluded, and hopefully drilled into your head, just how important being unique and building a social media fan base is by now. But that's what everyone is trying to do... so how do you accomplish that?

The first thing you do before you even start to think about management and record deals and fan-bases is figure out *exactly* who you are as an artist; what your sound and message is like and who your potential audience is going to be.

We think one of the reasons why nothing was working out for us at the beginning was because we were unsure of what path we were going to follow and what it was that represented us as artists. Once we got that down, that's when people became interested. We packaged ourselves in a way that appealed to the groups that we were trying to attract. Our imaging, media, presence online, and content were all consistent.

You can even sit down and have yourself a little brainstorming session and write things down on paper to help you make it all clear for yourself before you even do anything else. Once you've got who you want to be as an artist down pat, that's when you move onto bigger and better things.

Your sound and image should correlate and come together seamlessly with the demographic you're trying to target as an audience. With our style of music, if we started dressing up as punks and heavy metal rock-band types, trying to market ourselves to a bunch of people in that genre, they might be attracted to our look, but they'd totally hate us when they heard our music because that's not an accurate representation of our sound.

So to build a fan base, you begin by deciding what it is that truly depicts you as an artist and then you put it out there for people. Don't be shy or hesitant. Here's the thing: If you're doing a particular style of music and you have this specific sound, and you like it, we can guarantee there are a whole bunch of people out there in the world who like the same thing. You just have to connect with them. For example, with us, Lisa, Katherine, and Christina had been singing three-part harmonies since we were really young, so it was natural to stick with something that we already knew we were good at, plus it was different at the same time. How many artists can you name that solely sang a capella in this time and age? That was our sweet spot, and we ran with it!

On the other hand, if you find that you've got everything figured out and people still aren't biting, that does not in any way mean it's not good. It may not be totally marketable to a mass audience, but true artistry is inside your soul. Do whatever it is you feel made to do and fulfills you. Don't try to change just for mass appeal. Remember when we talked about purposeful segregation? You will do more appealing to those who your music *does* appeal to rather than trying to throw a dart on a huge board. Pick a smaller board, and be the biggest dart in the market.

Keep Working at It—It's Worth It

Once you're on your way, hang on for a long and bumpy ride! Just look at us: Christina has been working hard toward this almost since 2005. It was 2007 before Cimorelli even became a band and another two years till we blew up on YouTube. It's been a long time coming, and that's OK. It can take a long time for people to catch on and realize something good is right under their noses. We know it's frustrating, but that's how it goes. There will come a time when you'll get the exposure you're looking for; you just have to keep at it, not give up, and keep trying over and over and over again.

Even with building your social media presence, don't give up when it feels fruitless. Get out there and really get into people's faces and create that personal connection. That's the best possible way of building a fan base. It might take a while and be a slow and sometimes not so steady ride, but we collectively think it's entirely worth it.

For us, the slow build is much preferred to just being thrust into the limelight without having the chance to adjust to that change in lifestyle. Especially in this YouTube world, we've literally seen people who came out and up in the industry way after us, and as fast as they shot to the skies, they fizzled out just as quickly. They weren't ready for it and how fast it happened and really didn't know what to do with it because the building blocks weren't there to start with. They had the top rung of the ladder, but none of the others were there to hold it steady when they were at the top.

Being the lowest of the low and making it to the top makes you so much more aware and appreciative of all the good that ultimately comes from the hard work. We've always said that we wouldn't trade our uphill climb for all the shortcuts in the world. Not only does it keep you humble (coming from a place where no one knows you, and you constantly have to prove yourself over and over again just to be given a chance), but you learn to be that much stronger and confident as individuals and artists. It's great personal development.

You keep discovering your strengths, the ones you never thought you had, and the ones that get even stronger. It's quite surprising to realize that you can exceed your own expectations.

We've had to go through times where the only person in our audience was our aunt. Imagine standing in a huge area all set up for a performance we thought was going to be attended by quite a few people, and our aunt was the only one in the audience!

Even after we signed our record deal, on our first red carpet, we were getting yelled and screamed at to get out of the way and move because there were some big artists there and nobody wanted us in their way. That was harsh, but we put on our tough shells and survived!

That's why you can't chase this dream for the fame and to feed your ego and what other people think about you. That becomes a very dark hole in the entertainment industry, as we've seen so many times. You've got to do it for yourself and your own happiness. Then every negative thought; every sleepless, anxious night; and every single tear is worth it when you get to do something you're passionate about and that you love.

You Must Take Chances with Your Music

By the end of 2010, we'd built a fan following, and we were doing pretty great for ourselves. We had management at the time that was almost completely hands-off creatively, giving us full creative control to do whatever we thought fit; it was kind of perfect. That is until we tried to change it up a little.

Lisa was way into the music editing program Garage Band at the time, and we decided we'd been doing the same thing for a little bit, so maybe it was time to throw a little something different into the mix. Instead of doing another a cappella video, we prerecorded a video with instruments—a little piano and a little guitar—and we put it up.

We got so many negative reviews, it was insane. It even freaked our manager out, so much so, that she called and told us to take it down immediately. We didn't, because, well, we're too independent and stubborn at times, and we liked it! We just waited it out, and after 24 hours, the video blew up and got us the largest amount of views we had had yet!

That's why we say don't ever be afraid to try your hand at something new. You *must* keep evolving to keep people interested! Once we'd built a sufficiently big fan base, we wanted to branch out from doing just covers. It's always a gamble when you try to make the transition from covers to original music. You want people to know that you can do original music, but it's also scary throwing something out there and waiting for whatever reaction your hard work will receive. To save ourselves the mental torture, we used our covers to introduce people to our original music slowly and gradually at first. To accomplish that, we built a little bit of curiosity and momentum by teasing our audience before we actually released the music. You can do that, too, by adding little snippets of a new song or video at the end of the previous one. We do this whenever we're coming out with something new, and it works really well!

Whenever we've stepped out of our comfort zone and done something that our audience isn't used to seeing, it's always been met with the least amount of enthusiasm. But eventually, whatever it is, gets accepted and grows bigger than we initially thought possible, even given the harsh initial reception.

That exact thing happened when we did a choreographed dance routine to a cover we did of the hit song "Call Me Maybe" by Carly Rae Jepsen and when we collaborated with Matty B for a second cover of this same song. That video now has over 100 million views! Collaborations are *huge*, by the way! Even with touring, team up with another artist and set up a string of five or six shows around the state/region.

Every song that we've collectively been slightly hesitant about because it wasn't something that we normally went for initially was rejected completely and then went on to become an extreme success. That's the pattern of trends. This just shows that audiences as a whole are afraid to accept new things and adapt to change, yet you just have to push through, because if you like something and are targeting the right demographic, they will like it too. You just have to be persistent and patient.

Think about songs you hear on the radio that you may not like on the first listen. But you hear it a second and third time, and it really grows on you. Those songs don't get old as fast, and they usually do really well on the charts. They pave a new path sonically, so it takes a minute for your ears to adjust. It's the ones you usually can sing along to right away that you get sick of after about a week.

Don't Second-Guess Yourself

The most important thing is to find that niche where you just click. We found that YouTube worked the best, so we focused on building a foundation there and branching out. We don't try to dominate every platform; it's easy to get lost as a "floater" that way. We've gotten the highest number of followers on YouTube, and it's always been that way. It doesn't necessarily have to be the same for you, though. You can pick any social media network to capitalize on. For many, Instagram, Vine, or Twitter might be the bigger platform to reach out to the masses; for us, it's always been YouTube because that was our genesis.

If you're interested in tackling YouTube, first off, you should strategize and plan everything out in advance. If you're meticulous and detail-oriented, good for you...that should be right up your alley. However, if you're like us, who are more "let's just wing it and see how it goes" kind of people, then we have this to say: *Trust your instincts.*

If you feel like there's something that you should be doing or are curious about, go for it. Don't stop and second-guess yourself and question every tiny little thing and drive yourself insane. That's called "analysis paralysis," and it's the worst thing for progress. If you think you have a good idea, then it probably is one, so just go for it. It doesn't have to be perfect.

We're not only talking about when you're just starting. Even if you have a substantial following, don't question yourself when making decisions just because you're worried about how it's going to be received and perceived. It's better to put *something* out there than nothing! Bad press is still press! Of course, you *prefer* it be good press, so run with your best ideas first. Maybe even run it by a few friends to do some market testing and get some initial feedback.

We did a scripted web series with the writer of *Hannah Montana* one summer, for instance, and it went beyond our expectations! What's more, that "Summer with Cimorelli" web series really re-energized our fans in a way we didn't think possible. Our numbers on social media sites grew because a scripted series with all of us acting was really new and different and kept them interested!

Consistency without Overkill

Consistency is the key to making it big on social media. You cannot drop off for too long, because with the number of options available and the short attention span of the audiences, if you vanish for a long time, people tend to forget and just move on to other stuff. You don't want that.

This argument has a flip side, though. You can't be *too* consistent, if you know what I mean. Don't be that person who posts like eight pictures up on Instagram in an hour, every hour, or that friend you have on Facebook who must post a new status every 20 minutes. No one likes that!

If you're flooding people's inboxes over and over and over again, you're going to end up irritating them so much with your constant presence that even if they wanted to like your video or give positive feedback, they wouldn't because they're so tired of you being in their faces all the time. It's like when you think about that one person you know whom you assume is desperate because they text you all the time. Find the happy medium.

Join Forces: YouTube Video Collaborations

The beginning of Cimorelli started well before we ever posted our first YouTube cover, and while that may have been what put us on the map, just being a successful YouTuber has never been the end goal for us. Sure that's where our career took off, but we're branching out into the physical space and continuing to challenge ourselves with other things, like touring and more writing and recording. If you, however, have an ultimate goal of becoming a raging success on YouTube, video collaborations are a step in the right direction.

If you want to collaborate with an artist you admire, reach out to them. We were approached by Matty B to do a parody-collaboration, just because they liked our version of "Call Me Maybe" and thought it'd be a great idea to join forces. Some of us thought it was a terrible idea, but the others remained insistent, so we had to meet in the middle. Now it is our most-viewed video of all time!

Another piece of advice: Don't flat out just say no to an offer because you think nothing is going to become of it. There will be so many opportunities that will come your way; your job is to recognize them for what they are and just go for it. You can't get on your high-horse and refuse to work with someone who is up and coming, because you never know—they might be the next Matty B! As sensible Lisa always says, "not giving it a shot at all has a greater chance of ruining your career than taking a chance and saying yes." More often than not, you'll find, like we have on countless occasions, the things you least expect to turn out successful are the ones that do.

Take Advantage of YouTube Networks

There are YouTube networks that will sign you on and help you monetize (make money off) your YouTube channel with ads, partnerships, audience development, and cross-promotion, among other things. They will also help you connect with other YouTubers in a way that is mutually beneficial for your exposure. We were actually behind the curve on this and didn't know anything about this until it had already been three years since we'd been making covers on YouTube!

As with everything we did, except when picking our manager, we met with a bunch of different networks and then picked the one that stood out the most. We decided to go with We Are the Hits. Founded by Sony/ATV Music Publishing, We Are the Hits is an online network for musicians that monetizes cover songs.

If YouTube networks are something you might be interested in, you can easily reach out to these multichannel networks yourself. These companies are interested in supporting new and upcoming talent, so it doesn't matter if you have a significant number of views on your YouTube channel or not. You just approach them via their website, and they may sign you if they think you have potential and you show dedication and a growth plan. But do your research and be cautious about what you're doing; make sure it is a right fit for you. If you sign to a network, pay attention to the contract. Don't sign any contract "as is," as they are always very slanted toward the network's side; you can and should negotiate the terms with your lawyer and make sure you're willing to give up a percentage of your ad revenue.

Think of signing with a YouTube network the same way you would a label. There are pros and cons to partnering with any team. Contract terms you should investigate and negotiate include what they may be offering you, how long the contract is, if they're transparent with your earnings, and how they plan to promote you.

Just like a label, they won't do the heavy lifting. And the more attractive your content is, the more likely they will focus on you and help you grow your YouTube career.

Partner with a Brand to Build Your Audience

Partnering with brands is an incredible way to build a platform and increase visibility, and YouTube can help. YouTube shows you exactly the kind of demographic you are most popular with, which is pretty awesome. Once you know that, you can pick a brand (say Nike, Tractor Supply, Whole Foods, or something smaller) that caters to a similar demographic and approach them with a joint venture offer. Of course, you can't just approach them and say, "Hey, let's do something together." You need a well-put-together plan, with a very clear campaign, which includes the number of people and demographics you plan to reach. In other words, you need to make the case why it is good for *them*! You could approach them yourself, but it might be smarter to have your manager or someone else you feel comfortable with representing you reach out on your behalf so your pitch comes across as more official. You could be a great addition to their marketing plan. What have you got to lose? The worst that could happen is they'll say no.

Speaking of which, we have to let you guys in on a little secret here: A lot of "no's" can be turned into "yes's" just by being persistent and learning why you got the "no," and then adapting. Even if the answer stays a no, however, never burn a bridge and keep all names and contacts (you never know when they may come in handy).

After our first single got played on Sirius XM, we knew we were ready to approach the world of brands. We had a connection with Subway, which resulted in the scripted "Summer with Cimorelli" web series, and we even went on to do some commercials for them. Initially, the commercial wasn't on the table, but eventually it came about and really strengthened our image with our audiences because it gave us that official seal of approval.

We had the audience, we showed Subway how the collaboration could be beneficial to them, and we put together all the pieces to make it very easy for them to say yes. When it's your turn, carefully think through your proposal and remove or fix any reason the company would have to say no.

We hope our story and sharing the initiatives we have taken can be helpful to some of you. We are so blessed to be doing what we do, and we don't take it for granted for a single day. It's a difficult path, but if you are built to do music, you do it because you *have* to... it's not about the fame or fortune for us, and it never will be. We do it to connect with you, all of you out there who feel something from our music. We are cheering you on! Thanks for being a part of our journey!

Cimorelli
xoxo ♡

WE HANG OUT HERE

www.CimorelliMusic.com

Facebook: Facebook.com/Cimorelliband

Twitter: @CimorelliBand

YouTube: YouTube.com/Cimorellitheband

Instagram: @CimorelliBand

Snapchat: @itscimorelli

CHAPTER THREE

"The Marketer"

ADLEY STUMP

Becoming an Artistpreneur

In today's world, instant fame is seemingly more attainable than ever before. Reality shows enable artists to acquire thousands of new fans with just a few minutes of exposure. Adley Stump used the momentum created from her spot on Team Blake on Season 2 of NBC's The Voice *to launch not only a singing career, but other profitable ventures as well. Long after her time on* The Voice, *she has continued to grow her name by treating it like a business. In this chapter, she shares valuable tips about the entrepreneurial spirit that is the essence of being an independent musician today, discusses landing a strategic partnership with Nissan and Little Black Dress Wines, and shares how to score a publishing deal that will pay for your next record.*

I'LL BE HONEST, I'M NOT ONE OF THOSE PEOPLE WHO GREW UP WANTING TO SING SINCE I was a kid. I think I wanted to be a scarecrow or something until I was about 12. Then up until my senior year in college, I had absolutely zero idea what I wanted to do with my life.

I won't bore you with a lot of my backstory because I know that's not what you came here to read. But here are the basics.

My Rise to "Fame"

I grew up in Tulsa, Oklahoma, where I was a cheerleader, in student council, and was an extremely outgoing kid. I played guitar and loved music, but I never thought too much about singing, especially in front of anyone. I would write poetry and rewrite my favorite band's lyrics and occasionally try to write my own. I remember auditioning for a musical in high school because I was into acting. It was an eight-person cast for a musical called *The Fantasticks*. The day the casting results came out, I ran to see if I had made the cut, even though it was doubtful because there were only eight characters. Lo and behold, my name was listed! Right there in black and white, it said: "Adley Stump: Mute."

I was the *mute* in the musical.

So much for my singing career! It's laughable now (it was then too), and that play was a blast; I think I played a door or a fence, or something, and I held a stick that people would sing on either side of. A true star in the making!

I graduated from Bishop Kelley High School in Tulsa and went to Oklahoma State University to pursue a degree in public relations. I had cheered since I was five, but I decided not to cheer in college and focus on my sorority, Pi Beta Phi, and, ahem, classes. I worked for American Cheerleaders Association in the summers and enjoyed the heck out of college, but until my senior year, I had no earthly idea what I wanted to do for a career. I just knew what I was good at.

The summer before my senior year I took an internship with a non-profit called To Write Love On Her Arms. TWLOHA presents hope and finds help for people struggling with depression, addiction, self-injury, and suicide. My father was in the middle of losing his battle with alcohol addiction, so I had a huge passion for what they did. I moved to Cocoa Beach, Florida, for the summer, and there was this little dive bar that did karaoke on Tuesday nights. After work, the interns and I would roll down there, have a couple drinks, and get up and sing; we were just being goofy. No one there knew me and I had nothing to lose, so I would occasionally bring my guitar, get up there, and sing a few.

Performing wasn't new to me. I had been a performer my whole life with dance and cheer, but singing was a different animal. It was just me; there was no routine to hide behind. As far as confidence goes when performing, I learned a long time ago to "fake it until you make it." I found that if you *pretend* you're confident, you would ac-tually *become* confident over time. Or at least appear that way!

My goal at this point was to stay on with TWLOHA and do PR for them because they work with a lot of bands that represent the cause. Music was a huge part of the awareness. I could merge my love for music by promoting these bands and the mission of TWLOHA. With the internship under my belt, I went back to my last year of college having a little more interest in singing, but still never allowing myself to dream *that* big. After all, we know the odds, right?

In my sorority, we would partner with fraternities and do these shows: dancing, singing, etc. I had always been in charge of chore-ography for the shows I directed, since that was my background. I came back senior year and started singing more in those shows and even winning some solo parts.

But here is where things got interesting.

I was broke. And like most college students, Ramen noodles were my primary food group. So one day, I decided I wanted to go on *Jeopardy* and win some money. Side note: I'm smart, but I'm not *Jeopardy* smart. Most every success I've ever had in my life has come from the attitude and the choice to just try something and see what happens and not take myself too seriously. I don't believe in negative self-talk, and I can't surround myself with people who have that mentality. It's toxic to the success mentality in business and in life. You are the *only* person who can determine the quality of your future.

To prepare for the show, I Googled "How to be on *Jeopardy*," and a list of reality shows came up. I had missed the deadline for Jeopardy, but saw a show called *The Voice*. I was sitting with one of my sorority sisters, when she smacked me on the back and said, "Hey Ad, I dare you to try out for this show. Ha! You do karaoke good on Wednesdays when we give you Coors Lite!"

Challenge accepted.

A few weekends later, my boyfriend and I jumped in the car at 8 p.m. on a Friday and headed toward Nashville. That's where the audition was, and I had always wanted to see Nashville, so it was the perfect weekend road trip! I was scheduled to audition the next morning, so we chugged energy drinks and drove through the night. I clearly really cared about the quality of my voice, huh?

Long story short, I got the callback for Season 2, and I was set to head to LA for the Executive Auditions. I'm sure some of you are curious about this process, so I'll go into it a little. But first, let me tell you what was happening while I was waiting for the callback.

Don't Sign Random Record Deals (aka, Get a Lawyer)

I was performing for fun around Stillwater, Oklahoma, with my guitar player and right-hand man (still to this day) Andy Adamson. God bless him for bearing with me during this time. I didn't know what the heck I was doing; I was terrible! My mom had reposted a video of me and my friends making a music video where we decided all our scenes had to be shot in the guest bathroom. Don't ask...we were weird.

A friend of hers from high school had seen it and messaged her saying he dabbled in the music business and asked if I had a demo. My mom forwarded me his message, and he and I jumped on a phone call that evening.

We totally hit it off. We were both business-minded, faith-based individuals and felt like there was a good opportunity for us to work together. At the time, I still wanted to go do PR for TWLOHA and work in the nonprofit field in a cubicle somewhere. But he rolled it on thick and told me that I didn't belong behind a desk and I had talent. I knew stuff like this doesn't happen every day. We decided I should come up to Nashville and visit him and his family during my senior-year spring break.

We talked more and more in between then and graduation, and he presented me with a contract. I had a couple family members and adult friends look at it. They all said they obviously weren't music business experts, but this contract looked terrible and not in my favor at all.

I'll be the first to admit these were my honest thoughts: "I'm not going to get this opportunity again. This gets me to Nashville. This gives me a chance. I'm gonna be a star. I'll just sign it. He seems like a great guy. How bad can it be?"

Answer: *way bad.*

But how was I supposed to know? So I packed up and moved to Nashville the day after I graduated college to start my new life as a country music singer.

I won't go into all the details, and I will say they had an amazing home and I was treated very nicely. But once I signed on the dotted line, everything to do with the business and me being treated as an adult and making my own decisions was thrown out the window.

Basically, here was the deal:

- I was not allowed to go into Nashville and take meetings without him.

- I had a curfew (I lived with them).

- I signed away 100 percent of my publishing for no draw (aka money).

- The contract had no end date.

- I didn't own rights to my name.

- They agreed to fund a minimum of $40,000.

- I was paid nothing.

Cool. Great way to start off, Ad.

So needless to say, when *The Voice* came calling, it was the perfect blessing in disguise.

Advice for The Voice *(and Really Any Reality Singing Show)*

I know some of you probably have negative views about a "true artist" going on a reality show, and hell, maybe even look down on or don't have respect for me because of it. That's cool. But let me tell you why I believe it was the best thing I could have done for my career.

Going on a show like *The Voice* is *no guarantee* of fame. Once you get off, unless they pick up your options and sign you, you go back to where you came from. You *feel* famous because you just gained tens of thousands of followers in a night. But the next season is coming right behind you. That show provides millions of dollars' worth of marketing on your face, but it is 100 percent up to you to create value from that after you air. Most of my friends who got even further than I did have quit music or still work a day job to chase the dream. That's the reality. The only reason I'm still here is because of my own initiative creating opportunities, which I will go into after this next section.

The contract for all of these types of shows *is* scary. But I would not let that deter you from going through the experience as far as you can. You will meet amazing people to further build relationships with throughout your career, and that is irreplaceable. You take the risk, but 9 times out of 10, for most people, it's worth it.

So let me digress for a minute and speak to this aspect of the industry for those who are interested. (*Note: This is only my opinion and should be taken as such.*)

I'm sure things are changing with the processes as the seasons continue. For me, I was able to send in an audition online and try to get a designated time slot so I didn't have to stand in the cattle call. If you can still do this (at the time of this writing, you can), *do it*! Or, if you can, try to get a recommendation from someone who has an "in." As you know by now, the majority of this industry is relationship-driven, so recommendations or getting to know the casting directors personally, even a production assistant, is key and largely helps your chances of getting noticed and standing out. It's just like already knowing someone in a company you are wanting a job interview for.

For your song choice, do not sing an original song, and do not sing something that is insanely popular right now. Because that is what *everyone* will be singing. When I auditioned, I was waiting in the hall to go in, and one of the casting directors stuck their head out and said, "If you are even *thinking* about singing Lady Gaga, go home, or find a new song. We will not listen to any more Lady Gaga!" Because Gaga was on the blow up, everyone was singing whatever the song was that was popular of hers at the time. They want to hear something that makes their ears perk up, not a song they've already heard 100 times today.

Remember, I didn't know what the heck I was doing. I had big ol' hair, a big smile on my face, a memorable look (without looking crazy, look genuine), a crazy/funny story about actually intending to be on *Jeopardy*, and I sang the a cappella intro of Christina Aguilera's "Show Me How You Burlesque" and blended it into Johnny Cash's "Folsom Prison Blues." It was pretty rad!

And it worked. The best song choices I have seen usually:

- Take some balls (Christina was a judge my season).

- Are interesting and memorable.

- Relate to the genre you are in but have a unique twist.

- Take the original song, but make it your own. They want to see superstar *artist* qualities, not just a good karaoke singer.

When they have seen thousands of people, in that city alone, they are *only* going to think twice about someone who stands out. *I promise.*

I did *not* have the best voice of the day...not even close. I even messed up and sang the wrong words...probably at several points! But I laughed at myself and brushed it off, and kept going. If you mess up, it's not the end of the world! But if they're going to put you live on camera in front of millions of people, they need to know you are not going to fall apart (if, and when) something goes wrong. You have to know how to be professional, entertaining, and keep going. Not freak out, apologize a million times, or start crying. If you want a professional music career, you have to be a professional.

So...fast-forward to the Executive Auditions you go to if you get the call to go to LA. I can't say a lot about this because I'm pretty sure I signed some type of nondisclosure agreement, but in a nutshell, you sing two songs for that next audition. I sang Kenny Chesney's "You Save Me" and Carrie Underwood's "Last Name."

The process you go through is amazing. If you end up here, *get to know* the other contestants. You will learn and grow so much as an artist. Don't be a hermit. The wardrobe department will shop for you, you will go through a couple seminar-like things, and you will do interviews until your head falls off. It's awesome!

For those who make it past the Executive Auditions there are four days of blind auditions, where you appear on the actual show. This part is insanely nerve-wracking, as you can imagine, because you will be unable to hear how fast the teams fill up and how many slots are left. You can be out there all month, thinking and preparing for those 60 seconds on the show, and when it comes, you pray the teams don't fill up and your nerves don't get the best of you.

I auditioned on day three, and I was as scared as I've ever been in my life. Right before I went on, I remember watching from backstage as the four people in front of me *all* ended up on a team. I was thinking, "There is no way they will turn around for five people in a row!"

Remember, this was the biggest stage I'd sung on besides Willie's Saloon in Stillwater, Oklahoma. I was feeling way in over my head, and when my music started playing, I overshot my first note by probably three keys. Worst. Feeling. *Ever.*

I panicked and recovered, but my confidence was shot. I stared at the back of those chairs with a stare so intense it could have burned a hole through them. I was so focused on getting them to turn around that I had no soul to what I was singing. And you could tell. It was 10 seconds until the end of my performance, and no one had turned around.

I was talking to myself all defeated, saying, "Ad, it's OK, just *perform* now, do *you*, and walk off this stage proud of yourself." So I switched my focus and started performing to the crowd.

Boom! Right on my *last* note, Blake Shelton and Christina Aguilera hit their buttons. I went from the most defeated emotion to the most elated I have ever been in one instant. I about passed out. Not only did they turn around for me, but I made the show I'd thought about every moment for the last three months, I was on national TV, I was staring at two of my biggest idols and now I was expected to *talk* to them. Wildest feeling in the world!

Happily, I picked Blake. Then I babbled on about some nonsense I don't remember. I walked off stage, everyone was high-fiving me, someone handed me a digital camera, and then I was trying to catch my breath because Christina Milian was trying to ask me where I was from and tell me that she liked my hair.

Next we began filming the battle rounds. On my season we did not have all these other rounds like knockout rounds, or steals or swaps, etc. There was no trading teams or being saved, either.

Kelly Clarkson was my mentor on Blake's team. Needless to say that experience was breathtaking—and singing in front of her was petrifying.

I went to "battle" with a good friend I had gained over the three-month experience, named RaeLynn. Many of you may know RaeLynn now as she is out there kicking major butt with one of the best teams in the industry today.

I unfortunately cannot say a lot about this process and the behind the scenes of what goes on, but here is where my journey on *The Voice* came to an end, as RaeLynn won our battle. And look what an amazing career it has launched for her!

This battle had *massive* reviews and articles circling around it...it landed me on the front page of Yahoo, Billboard, and several other media outlets. I still have all those clippings, and I am able to use them today as part of my electronic press kit (EPK). *The Voice* was the No. 1 show in America that season, and the publicity torch that was lit from that battle was just enough for me to try to start a wildfire.

Back Home to Nashville

During my time in LA taping the show and being cooped up in the hotel with incredible artists for months, I learned a lot. We would talk about each other's dreams, careers, what was going on, etc. When I started to share details about my record deal, I realized something was really wrong.

I started to understand what I had signed would cripple me from ever making money or having a real career. Here I was getting all this publicity, and I wasn't going to be able to do anything with it!

When my time on *The Voice* ended and I was back in Nashville, I tried to reason with my investors and the deal that was in place with their company. Reasoning with traditional business-minded people in an industry that is anything but is an uphill battle. They didn't understand. They wanted quick returns, and a career or investment in the music industry is anything but.

They wouldn't listen to me or hear of me changing any of their crazy rules. I can't work with people like that, and I can't work with disrespect. So I started trying to find a way out after a month or so of getting nowhere with them and no glimpse of compromise on their end. People in town were refusing to work with me if I stayed attached to them.

Now, I'll be totally honest about what happened next. I found a lawyer, Robin Gordon, on Music Row (after calling and telling my story to probably twenty others) who said he would help me, with no money upfront by the grace of God. Robin was a godsend and so kind during my biggest time of need. We tried and tried to negotiate with them. They had invested about $40,000, and wouldn't settle for less than $2 million and royalties for the next ten years or something crazy. I'd make a pitcher of margaritas for the lawyers and interns every time we had to go over a new offer. That made it much more tolerable and lighthearted, as this obviously was *not* a fun time.

Robin eventually told me after a month or so, "Listen, Ad, you have a ton of debt now. You can fight this guy in court and be held up for eighteen months with probably a crappy deal at the end and lose all your momentum, or you can file bankruptcy and be done in three months and walk free and clear."

Obviously, neither are fun options, but I had gotten myself into this deal, and it was a hard lesson. I was upfront and told the investors/ record company what I would have to do if they would not strike a deal with me. And granted, we had made them a sweet offer; I am still baffled (yet thankful) they didn't take it. I was saddened that this man was so greedy and blinded by his misguided faith and ego that he was going to force a 22-year-old girl to file bankruptcy just so she could make a living. He turned down my final and best offer, so I had no choice but to file for bankruptcy, to rid myself of a lifetime of future financial obligations to him.

I have quickly built my credit back, and it was definitely the right choice for me, but I knew I needed to act fast and act smart to keep up momentum from *The Voice.*

Know Your Business

There are a million different paths to success. What works for some will not work for others. I am not a lifer on the road like Cody Canada. And I am not a hot teenage boy who can get millions of screaming fans to do whatever I say because I'm 14 and have abs. I have to look at my best qualities and my quickest way to maximum results with the minimal effective dose, or MED. Tim Ferriss, author of the book *The 4-Hour Workweek*, teaches a lot about MED, and it has completely changed the way I operate as a self-employed person. What is the minimum effective dose needed to get the results you desire? If you can get the basics of running Pro Tools down in 5 days to lay down a sample track, don't spend 15 days and drive yourself crazy.

Water boils at 212 degrees. You can heat it to 275 if you want to but you aren't making the water "more boiling." You are just wasting resources. Focus on where *your* time is best spent and go all chips in there.

There is a huge difference between being busy and being productive. Learning the keys to efficiency and quality in any business will benefit you greatly. In music, it will especially set you apart if you know how to treat yourself like a business and operate effectively and with a plan. Before you go to bed, I suggest you write down the top four things you need to get done the next day—two big things and two small things. To do this, you will have to set specific goals based on what you want to achieve in life, and reverse engineer how to get that done. By setting a daily plan for yourself, you will make gradual, yet measurable, advances toward attaining your goals.

One of my assets I used off the bat was my hair. Whether people loved it or hated it, they knew me because of it. One of my favorite stories is from a few days after my blind audition aired. I was at the gym, waiting in the line to go into Zumba. I could tell these girls in the line were looking at me and talking about me. One of them leaned over and said, "Wow, you wear your hair *just* like that girl on *The Voice*!

I started to laugh and say something back, but she started in again: "Well, you probably just wear it like that because you saw *her* do it," then she rolled her eyes.

It was awesome. Totally awesome. Her friend hit her on the arm and said, "You dummy! That *is* the girl from 'The Voice'! I'm so sorry!"

I laughed and said, "It's all good," and asked the girl to teach me her awesome Zumba moves for retribution.

I can't tell you how many times I was recognized, called out, made fun of, or whatever due to my hair. But because of this, I immediately partnered with Melissa Ahonen from BBT Style who makes her own custom hair accessories out of her home in North Dakota. We connected on Facebook when she offered to make me a custom headband. We launched "The Adley Stump Collection" of couture headbands and wraps, and we rode that train of creating passive income for the next year. I would order a set number of each design from her at a wholesale price and sell them at my shows and online. I would make a percentage of what she sold from the line as well, and she would pay me each month. I knew jumping on the road with a high pay rate was only going to last a few months, so I focused my efforts on things that would pay me residually and aid in brand building as well as be scalable after the next season or two passed. The headband line was carried in over thirty boutiques nationwide. That increased my brand exposure and leverage more at the time rather than trying to play shows a million places at once and spend a ton of money I didn't have self-funding a tour. People knew the hair. I didn't know how to fund a tour. It was the best thing I could have done at the time to build a small platform to work off of. Heck, we could have even done a tour and signings in the boutiques if we wanted to!

My entire career thus far (a little over three years as of writing this) has been focused on not bringing up and equalizing my weaknesses, but focusing on *my strengths* and what makes me unique—nothing else.

You would never tell your best friend, "Tammy! You have to come see this girl! She is kind of good, but like, at everything!" However you *would* say, "Tammy! You gotta see this girl; she can sing her butt off!" Or "She plays guitar like a mad woman and her live show is insane!" Whatever it is for you, whatever you enjoy the most, be better than everyone else. Outsmart them and outwork them, and do not give up when you hit a wall. Obstacles are there to show you whether you *really* want this dream, or you just thought you did.

Lessons Learned

Going forward in this chapter, I will share a few stories that have been pinnacles in my career up to this point and gained me the most momentum and attention. Some of these ideas may not apply to you at all. But, hopefully, they will remind you that with that right plan and creativity, you *can* work outside the box, and eventually help you forget there is even a box at all.

Holding Out for the Right Team

After getting out of that terrible record deal, I was determined to not sign another contract and lock myself into a team unless I knew it was right. A few management teams approached me, but none were right for me. As good as it felt and as badly as I wanted someone to help brainstorm and take the load off my shoulders, I knew that if I signed a deal on a "lower-level," for lack of a better term, I would remain a "lower-level" artist, at least from what I was seeing in Nashville. I had heard talk of how important it is to not be contractually bound when you meet the *right* person because if you're tied up with a manager, a publishing deal, etc., it's much harder for that *right* person to take you and work with you.

Will this new guy have to buy you out of that deal, work with the person you signed on with who is dead weight, etc.? You never know. So for me, my strategy became to stay on my own, work alongside those who guided me through the industry and believed in me, create as much value as I could, but not sign anything that could cripple me unless I *knew* it was right.

I would work myself up the ladder, build leverage, get a bunch of good stuff happening on my own, and attract the type of people I wanted to work with. Then I would have the ball in my court, making a living on my own terms, plus have something attractive to offer them and show them what I had pulled off on my own.

Enter Joe Diffie.

Stealing Joe Diffie's Car

During my time on *The Voice*, I was worried I was going to be typecasted as "the cheerleading sorority girl who didn't know she could sing." While that was true, it was not the image I wanted. Out of the hundreds of interviews we seemed to do, they aired only 30 seconds, so I was terrified they were going to choose a clip that showed me being ditzy or "blonde" or whatever, which would become my image. So just in case, I started this YouTube series called "Get Stumped with Adley Stump." I'd get a camera crew and go around Nashville and "stump" people with these funny, random acts of kindness as a way to be able to show people more of my humor and my heart. This turned into being a unique platform for me that has helped me build a brand and showcase my best qualities as not only a singer, but also a "personality" and entertainer. So when it came time to release new music, this was something we incorporated.

As an independent artist, it's *so* important to think about how you can *naturally encourage the acquisition of new fans*, and be a *seamless addition* to how they consume their content. Don't interrupt it and demand their attention because you think you deserve it. I see so many artists spamming people on Facebook and Twitter saying, "Hey, I play guitar, like my page." Or "Hi, go buy my album." Not the best look. You've got to get creative and *earn* the fans you get. Are you a funny guy? Be funny online! Do you go on a lot of cool adventures? Post the pictures, and stay regular with it to build an identifiable brand image for yourself. *Draw* people to you, don't beg them for favors.

One of the ways we aimed to do this was with the launch of my single "Like This." I was trying to find a way that would encourage my existing fans to *want* to share my single with their friends and family instead of me begging them to spread the word and being overly self-promoting. I thought, "What is something everyone would want to see someone do?" So I came up with "steal a country music star's car."

Hell, I would love to see someone do that!

So I posted on Twitter that I would steal a country music star's car and videotape it if my last tweet about my single got over 100 retweets.

Boom! Retweets were phenomenal (as were sales, consequently), and I was a tad overwhelmed by the response. But that was exactly what I wanted. Then the reality set in...crap, I *actually* have to steal a celebrity's car!

I brainstormed celebrities I knew or people I had a connection to that wouldn't get *too* pissed off. Longtime country-music star Joe Diffie and I had become friends through my boyfriend who had restored a clock for George Jones that Joe had given to him. Joe had taken us to dinner a few months back, and told us he was getting a new truck. Bingo!

I spent the week preparing to steal Joe's car, but in everything you do, you want to think of how you can extend the marketing reach as far as possible. If you're doing a show, can you record it live and print CDs on the spot to sell from that show? Can you stream it live online for a discounted ticket price? Can you upsell VIP wristbands for a meet and greet? If you're pursuing a beverage sponsor and are in a strong market for them, tell them you'll include their product in the VIP area and pass out free drinks to fans when they come backstage. They're usually pretty good about giving away product if it makes sense for them and you keep *their* goals in mind when asking for something. Reaching out to brands and building relationships is a numbers game, but it's also a strategy. More on this later...

Knowing the amount of press stealing Joe's car could garner, and letting a few key bloggers know the information ahead of time, I wondered if I could turn this into the biggest "Get Stumped" episode to date. People knew I was going to steal a celebrity's car, but they didn't know what I secretly planned to do with it. That was what I could turn into a humorous act of kindness, which was the message of "Get Stumped."

All this was going down right after the devastating tornadoes in Moore, Oklahoma. I knew several devastated families, so what I wanted to do was find a family who was in desperate need of a vehicle, steal Joe's brand-new Nissan Titan, make the swap with another new Nissan Titan (hopefully one donated by a charitable Nissan dealer), and give it away to that family.

When something that terrible happens, your heart breaks. You want to do anything you possibly can to help those whose lives were just torn out from under them in a matter of minutes. I couldn't write a check, I couldn't rebuild their homes or bring their loved ones back, but I *could* write a song. I *could* donate every dollar from sales to the relief efforts, and I *could* try to help them emotionally get through their worst nightmares. And *maybe* I could get Nissan to help.

So with that, I contacted the dealership I bought my Nissan Cube from. I called my friend there and told him what I was doing, the amount of press I planned to get, and the impressions (people who would see it) that I had estimated. To put together this pitch for Nissan, I called my friend Rick Walker who ran Imagine PR to ask if he would help me put together a press packet and sponsorship kit. We did all the thinking for Nissan by creating a complete plan, so all they had to say was yes. We covered all our bases.

We put a plan together to steal Joe's car and bring in another celebrity to kick off the hashtag "#wheresadley" on Twitter. It would be a three-day social media goose chase. People would watch me steal the car, but then it would keep going. I would stop at six different Nissan dealerships across three states heading toward Oklahoma, and we would do radio and TV remotes at each one to get even more press across this half of the country. I would take pictures of me in random locations with Joe's hijacked truck and let people try to find us. I would bring a camera crew with me to film every bit of it, and afterward, turn it into a "Get Stumped" episode that could be replayed for anyone who had missed it, extending the life of the giveaway and bringing awareness to what people in Oklahoma were going through.

We had this nicely laid out in a packet I sent to my Nissan friend, and he ran it up the flagpole for me. Rick and I jumped on countless conference calls with Nissan corporate, and we had prepared an answer to any question they might have. They closed the deal with us in three weeks. I contacted a Moore firefighter to help me find a family that was in the deepest need for this vehicle, since he had his ear to the ground during the devastation.

We were off to the races.

I showed up at Joe's house with a camera crew the following week, telling him I was taping for a reality show (I had to explain the cameras). His management and wife knew I was coming, so they told him to go outside and wash his truck. We started chatting and I awkwardly asked him if I could take it for a test drive. He agreed because he couldn't really say no since we had him on camera.

Little did he know I wasn't coming back. Somehow, we pulled everything off the next three days without a hitch. There were so many small details to work out, but I had a team with me on the road that had a heart to help, and I couldn't have done it without them.

The fireman I worked with had found us the Candelaria family who had lost their home, their cars, and their *child* in the tornadoes. I contacted them, told them who I was, and told them Joe and I (both Okies) wanted to do something for them. I asked Hideaway Pizza to sponsor a meal for us as we came through, and we timed it with Joe's concert in Oklahoma City...once Joe figured out what was going on when I didn't come back with his truck. So the Candelaria family and I met at Hideaway, had a meal, talked, and shared many, many tears. I told them I was taking them backstage to Joe's concert. They had no idea I would actually pull them up onstage mid-show to tell them what we had actually been up to the last three days and that they were going home in a new truck.

The entire arena became emotional, as several of the audience member's homes had been devastated as well. It was one of the most moving moments of my life. If you want to see all of it, you can watch "Get Stumped," Episode 5, on YouTube.

Creating Passive Income and Fan Growth

One of the most frustrating things in this business is the "hurry up and wait," but it's inevitable. It takes time to build a career, but you don't want to waste valuable time waiting for an answer from some suit behind a desk. I want to be in charge of my own future, so I tend to keep about six projects shuffling (making sure they all cross-promote each other) at all times, to not only keep myself from going crazy, but also to make sure I'm always moving forward and keeping momentum when something doesn't happen that I was really hoping would.

One of the ways I tried to keep money coming in was by setting up a system for acquiring new fans, retaining them once I had their attention, and understanding my cost per fan. I learned how to do this from a guy named John Oszajca.

If you aren't familiar with John, he is known for several things, but showing artists how to make money and gain new fans is probably my personal favorite. John created a system called Music Marketing Manifesto.

howtheysellmusic.com/mmm

MMM walks artists step by step through the process of creating a *system* to actually sell your music. Just telling people you have an album and they should buy it probably doesn't have the conversion rate you're looking for. And it's not because you're not any good or you haven't had enough exposure. It's because you don't have a system that shows your fans exactly what you want them to do.

I spent two to three weeks building my system with the help of John's courses, and it has 100 percent changed the relationship I have with my fans, for the better. I learned so much more than I could have in two years of trying to do this on my own. Not to mention I am making more money. Every day I'll get a notification or two that pops up telling me I sold a new product.

Now I have a fantastic way of growing my relationship with fans that *I control*, unlike social media mediums that are always changing the way you can interact with your fans. I'll let you check it out for yourself, but it is definitely one of the best things I have done to make a living in the new music business and stay self-employed, so I wanted to share it with you.

howtheysellmusic.com/mmm

Relationships Are Everything

You never know where relationships will lead you, and you never know who is watching. It's truly incredible.

Case in point: I was in Kentucky one day shooting a Hyundai commercial. (I'm pretty sure I found the job on Craigslist, no lie. You never know.), when I got a call on set from a random Los Angeles number and I answer it.

It was Taylor Armstrong from the *Real Housewives of Beverly Hills*.

Cue: peeing my pants on set.

Taylor was my babysitter while I was growing up, and my mom was her cheerleading coach. But we hadn't really spoken since! She told me she loved my cover of "Hallelujah" she got on iTunes and that she was getting married in two weeks and would like me to sing it as she walked down the aisle.

You're kidding me!

I agreed and was at her wedding two weeks later. It turned out it was being nationally televised on David Tutera's wedding planning show *CELEBrations. Nice!*

It was a very small industry wedding, but I sang as she came down the aisle, sang her first dance song with my buddy Josh Tatum, and ended up singing with Taylor and the band the majority of the night. When I got off stage, her agents Steve Small and actor/comedian Jamie Kennedy (of Artist to Artist and Jamie Kennedy Entertainment) handed me a card and said we needed to talk. So did her publicist. The right crowd, the right performance, the right confidence...it was just *right*.

From what I knew of these guys, I knew I was ready to pull the trigger with them after several conversations following that night. I have been with them ever since for the TV/film aspects of my career.

Another example of relationships at work is my recent deal with Little Black Dress (LBD) wines. I got this opportunity through an angel of a friend, who is a music promoter and wine blogger. Eric worked for them and proposed a plan to partner with an up-and-coming artist. Although he recommended me, the crazy part was we had never even met in person. He just knew of me from Twitter and had seen what I'd done over the past two years. I had no idea who he was or what he did.

The endorsement deal was between me and a friend of mine. But I wanted this, and I knew I could create a set of deliverables that would be pretty strong. So I did what I had done for the Nissan deal and took the time to write out a packet of ideas, which included bringing in other celebrity friends to post about the wine at events I put on, doing social media takeovers with my celebrity friends and LBD, getting radio to do remotes at shows LBD had me playing (so it was sort of a paid-for radio tour), and placing QR codes on their labels with exclusive music downloads of a song I would write (and license) to them.

I wanted to show LBD I would be doing more than just putting their name on my banners and mentioning them in interviews. I would be using their budget to create items that revolved around memorable *moments* and ensured deeper return on investment for their brand. For example, I pitched creating light-up wine charms with their brand and my name on them to hand out at the shows, each one a different color for a different varietal of wine. The audience, women especially, would have fun picking out what color they wanted based on what they drank. I would invite audience members to turn on the charms when I sang a certain song in my set. Then they'd take the charm home and use it again and again. Events like this locked them into the brand much more than me just "thanking my sponsors" or having their name displayed at my merchandise table.

If you want to approach a sponsor when you don't already have them, these are the kinds of deliverables you need to create and offer.

When Eric told me they were interested in jumping on the phone with me, as well as the other artists in the running, so they could narrow it down, I looked at what *they* wanted to accomplish. They wanted to sell more cases of wine. So I wrote plans to fit that and they appreciated it deeply. Again, I made it very easy for them to just say yes. LBD is an incredible wine with a fantastic heart for some beautiful charities. Our partnership is fun, proactive, and a win-win for both parties as we work on national promotions to leverage both our audiences.

Sometimes You Have to Create Your Own Opportunities

And as you all know, it takes money to move forward in this industry, and it requires a heck of a lot of overhead. I had hit a dry spot—the touring season was slowing down and I hadn't released new music in a while—so no money was coming in. What do you do in situations like this? Create your own opportunity!

I was sitting at Jason's Deli one afternoon eating a salad and brainstorming ways to create a paycheck for myself for the next six months until the LBD sponsorship would kick in. I was texting a friend of mine, Jessica, who is an NFL marketing agent. We were cut from the same cloth as far as our intense work ethic and love for creating deals. We had said before we'd love to do something together some day. Our conversation that day went something like this:

> *Me:* "I'm eating salad at a restaurant by myself. This is a new low. What are you doing?"
>
> *Jessica:* "Plotting world takeover while drinking a Corona. Duh."
>
> *Me:* "Proud of you. I'm outlining blueprints for financial masterminding in my ranch dressing."
>
> *Jessica:* "Write me in."

Hmmm.

> *Me:* "Ever thought of doing something in music?"
>
> *Jessica:* "Don't know. What do you have in mind?"

(Pause) I've got nothing.

Cue, *figure it out!*

What are my assets? What am I doing that she can easily be involved in that won't suck up her time? How can I make us both money? If someone approaches you with an open-ended offer, make them an offer a bit higher than you normally would and let them negotiate you down. You don't want to undercut yourself, but be reasonable.

I quickly ran through all the scenarios in my head:

- I knew I was about to be working on this new single and album to support the distribution with Little Black Dress.

- I knew how tough getting a decent publishing deal was in Nashville, which was time I didn't have.

- I knew I wouldn't be 100 percent focused on writing new music after the next six months when I had the album done.

- And I knew I didn't want my publishing tied up for a long time with someone not in the music industry that could hinder future deals.

Bingo—I had it!

I offered Jessica a project-based publishing deal. It was perfect: short-term investment, long-term return on investment. Here's how I pitched it to her:

> *Me:* I am 100 percent focused on writing for the next six months for this album. I'll offer you my publishing on it. If you've ever thought about dipping your feet into publishing, you know that it's a $2 to $3 million investment with no expected returns for a minimum of three years. You're talking hiring staff, writers, pluggers, admin, and paying for demo sessions, all just hoping to get a cut with an artist.
>
> But this deal is directly with the artist (me). You've got every cut on the record, plus what I don't cut, we can pitch to other artists. I've got distribution in x, y, z, and I can get you $1,000 back guaranteed in the first month (Little Black Dress was going to pay to license my single). I'll draw you up a one-pager and send it over this afternoon.
>
> *Jessica:* "Do it."

I literally wrote that out while I was eating an ice cream cone, making it up as I went. But it made sense to me. Why not do a project-based deal that guarantees them a return *and* gets me paid for what I'm already going to be doing? The key was that I had guaranteed partners and sales. You have to have something to offer and a way to get it out there above just putting it on iTunes. There's very limited money there; we're not trying to screw anyone out of getting their investment back. Think of what you do have or what you can create that would be a good business plan to offer someone if this is a path you want to go down. Everyone's situation is different; it may take years to build your assets, but remember, it's a marathon, not a sprint.

When it came down to discussing my advance, I threw out a number that was double the salary and half the terms most of my friends were making in their publishing deals—plus, I was able to continue co-publishing after recoupment. Bingo!

Whatever Makes You Unique—Use It!

Listen, I *love* business. Most artists don't, and that's totally fine. It's a strength for me, so I use it, and it just so happens to be a refreshing quality to see a female musician who knows what she's going for and has a plan to get there.

If you don't like business, don't focus on it. But know enough to hold a conversation and give people faith in you. Use what *you* have that's unique.

I don't have mad guitar playing skills, so I don't talk about that. I can't make sick beats, so I don't spend my time trying to learn to be mediocre at it. I spend my time growing my writing, my visibility (by *consistent* content output; you may get tired of hearing this by the end of this book, but it's so important!), creating deals, and networking with decision makers and influencers.

I was able to put this skill to good use once again while I was waiting for my lawyer to draw up the contract for Jessica's deal. I went to a newlywed party with my family in Maryland. I was swamped with work (including the formation of this book) and was in *no mood* to go mingle with strangers. Which is rare for me, but I was exhausted.

I went with my family anyway, and it was a great time. I hit it off with the dad of the bride, Tom. He said his family came to Nashville often because he sat on the board of three health-care companies in town. This got us started talking about business.

Before I left the party, I exchanged numbers with Tom and his wife. He and I would text about every other day about business and taxes and weird stuff that I find interesting. He was so smart, and I crave being around people I can learn from—no matter what it is.

I told him about the publishing offer I had put together that Jess took me up on and what I was working to bring to the table. He kept asking questions about it...and then he offered me $500 more a month if I would do it with him instead.

Holy crap! I didn't know what to do! I called Jess and told her about the deal. I explained that she and I would work on several projects in entertainment down the line, but this was probably the only way I could ever work with Tom and I really wanted to learn from him.

She was fine with it, and I love her for it, especially because we now have a few side ventures together in the sports and entertainment world. We know the strengths of each other's relationships, and we stay in contact daily as new things come across our paths.

Tom influences a lot of large groups that could be very beneficial for bulk album sales which was key to me building leverage. It's nontraditional to have a publishing deal with him, as he is not inside the music industry. But I had a feeling we could do something unique, and I had learned enough in my last deal to know how to not get screwed again. Tom was fired-up passionate about it, and my gut trusted him. I believed this was the beginning of something great. So I negotiated a co-pub deal my lawyer still says is the best publishing deal he has ever drawn up. The deal is incredibly beneficial for both

PRO TIPS

MARKET YOUR BRAND

- *You can't market yourself if you don't know exactly what you are and who your audience is.* If you were a toy company, you wouldn't make a toy and just say, "Oh, it's for everyone. We'll just make it and put it out there and people will love it." No way! You know your distribution model, your audience...etc. You're a business, so you have to think like one.

- *Create a master calendar that shows consistent content output and milestone goals for your marketing initiatives.* What are you putting out every week, this month, the next six months, this year; and what *are* the goals that content is helping you work toward? You need to be more specific than just "I want to gain more followers on Instagram." Put a number to it, then figure out a way you're going to hit that.

- *Does your music stand out when turned down low?* Many industry A&Rs will turn on pitched music low in the background while they're working. They only bother to consider the ones that catch their ear and make them go turn it up. Is your music that hooky? Make sure your music can pass the test.

parties. The agreement keeps us protected and provides both of us with strong options for financial growth, yet allows me control of my career by giving Tom the rights to *revenue*, but not my master record-ings. Plus, we can re-up if we want when the six-month term is over.

That day I had told God that if He could help me create a paycheck for myself to pay the next few month's rent, I would be in pure shock. Leave it to Him to give me double what I had asked for.

Your luck (and luck is a huge part of it) in this industry is built largely off how you treat people, how well you create value, and how long you persevere.

Work Like No One Will Hand You Anything

It scares me how much I have left to learn. And I hope I get to keep learning forever. My hope is that *you* may have learned even one thing from these stories and the artists in this book that you can apply. We are all different in our artistry, and there is no "right" and no "wrong" way to do things. I have learned a lot the hard way, and I have more failed ventures than I have successful ones. But every one of those failures got me closer to pulling off the ones that worked.

If you are walking from your house to your work, and you fall flat on your face halfway, you are still not back at your house. You're *still* halfway there. Get back up and keep walking.

One of the best things I have learned and applied to my journey is to quit asking God to bless what I am doing, and start *doing what He is blessing*. Whether you believe in God or not, this is a fantastic principle that applies to not only our industry as artists, but life in general. You can push so hard in one direction and nothing seems to happen. Then you get a little lead in something weird or different, follow it and—*bam!*—the floodgates open. It happens more than you'd think—if you learn to follow little leads in new directions, rather than push for years on the same door that won't open. Maybe the back door is open. When you start recognizing problems as opportunities, everything will change provided you take the initiative to act on the solution.

I remember lying on the abs mat at the gym my first couple months in Nashville, just feeling overwhelmed with moving here. I had *planned* to be in PR. I had *planned* to work in nonprofit. I had *planned* to be writing blogs and promoting bands. Four months later, I was in Nashville, with a record deal, and about to be on national TV, and I was a *singer*. I felt like I had no tools and no preparation.

I asked God what the heck He thought He was doing. I had no idea how to succeed as an artist! Gratefully, I asked Him why He had given me so much opportunity in this direction and told Him I had just wanted to speak and encourage and inspire people. I felt like God smacked me upside the head and said, "Ad, I just gave you a stage and a microphone and a voice out of nowhere. What do you *think* you're supposed to do with it? You're not just supposed to 'sing songs.' Go move people. Go to work."

And work, I will.

There are so many small stories I could share along the way, but we'll have to save those for another time. Or feel free to hit me up on Facebook, Twitter, Instagram, or Snapchat to stay in touch and continue the conversation.

Thanks for reading, and I look forward to getting to know you all and your stories as we live this crazy journey together.

Don't be a stranger!

Yours in Music and Success,

CHAPTER FOUR

"The Creator" $

ANDREW BELLE

Beyond the Radio—
Songwriting for Film and TV

Andrew Belle is a deep thinker and a true believer in the art and craft of songwriting. In addition to winning over major soundtrack audiences with songs featured in Grey's Anatomy, Pretty Little Liars, *and* Vampire Diaries, *Belle also won the John Lennon Songwriting Contest...and topped that off with MTV's award for Best Breakout Artist in 2009. Andrew retraces his steps detailing how he found, and continues to find, success on and off the big screen.*

Note: Written by *How They Sell Music* and adapted from our "video chapter" with Andrew. As seen on *howtheysellmusic.com*

YOU COULD PROBABLY TRACK ANDREW'S LOVE AND APPRECIATION FOR MUSIC BACK to the '90s when the Counting Crows dominated the radio waves. Discovering their "August and the Everything After" record in the eighth grade was a game changer that led Andrew to become interested in *playing* music, rather than just listening to it. It made him want to approach his dad, who had a twelve-string guitar, and ask him to teach him everything he knew about playing music. Dad happily obliged.

"I started playing a little bit of music with my friends in high school, just gathering around and teaching each other different chords," Andrew says. "I was always the guy in the background. I played back-up guitar and *maybe* some scattered background vocals here and there. I never wanted to be the front man or a solo act."

He left that role to the other guys. "I've always been shy and just enjoyed letting other people shine." Andrew didn't even get around to songwriting until he was almost 20 and in college. And singing? Well, that came much later.

In Andrew's freshman year of college at Taylor University, he and his buddies took a road trip one week from Indiana to Chicago to see Dashboard Confessional in concert. A band called Brand New was opening for Dashboard, and while he had never heard of them, that 60-minute set was absolutely captivating. By the time he got back to campus, Dashboard was off the playlist, and Jesse Lacey, the lead singer of Brand New, had taken their place.

Listening to and studying Lacey's songs like crazy prompted Andrew to try his own hand at songwriting.

The ability to pair words with music, there's no other word to describe it other than magical. Being creative and poetic, expressing your emotions and thoughts in that new and vulnerable way is scary, yet inexplicably rewarding at the same time. Then watching it come to life in a recording, and then playing it live? He became addicted to it.

Find Your Groove

Andrew quickly founded his own band and began seriously working on his own songs, studying everything he could about the craft. As cool as the whole college rock band scene was, being in a band is not as easy as it's made out to be. So in his senior year of college, the realization came that he didn't want to attach his future to a group of people with different personalities and egos who may be there in the moment, but might not want the same things a couple years down the line when it's time to step into the real world. Going solo would potentially give him the best shot at success—and that's exactly what he did.

In the last semester of his senior year (with the help of a friend and his mostly unused recording equipment), Andrew recorded ten to twelve of the songs that were his pride and joy at the time. Although now he claims they are "cringe-worthy." But that's the goal as a songwriter, isn't it? If you think you have already written your best song, and you can never beat what you have, you may as well stop right now. You grow and change and get better.

When it came to change and chance, Andrew was leading the pack. Going from the background guy to the "face guy" was a huge change. Never taking voice lessons, never having sung in front of people, Andrew was comfortable as the guy strumming the bass in the background. But you don't get to be a success by being comfortable. Being front row and center requires a certain level of confidence that he wasn't even close to having.

But he was willing to try.

So he started playing in cafes around his college town, thinking it was a good way to get his feet wet and practice. "I can remember, very clearly, a few occasions of unattractive flailing around, trying to look cool. It definitely took me a while to find my own persona on stage and a *lot* of practice," Andrew says. "But I was determined."

Live performance has become the most viable stream of revenue for traditional artistry; it can't be replaced. But now, artists are expected to have so many extra qualities on stage; dancing, singing, being funny, speaking well, etc. It's a lot of pressure! There were no anecdotes or jokes between songs when composers and musicians performed hundreds of years ago. But with the star culture that's been created, audiences are increasingly tougher to please, and there is a level of expectation that is difficult to live up to. You're constantly expected to be funny and attractive and present a whole pretty little package, and not everybody is able to do that.

Many artists find this part of pursuing music the most daunting. "Try letting yourself off the hook a little bit," says Andrew. "You don't have to be the comedian or the most charming person in the world. Just start with playing your songs really well, in a way that transcends the need to put on a fake show, or anything that isn't inherently *you*. Hopefully listening to you sing will be the main reason people bought the tickets in the first place. So focus on that perspective, perform well, and let your music and talent speak for you. Once you've had a sufficient amount of practice, you can start to venture out of your shell and grow your comfort zone. Where I feel some artists make a mistake is trying to get outside their comfort zone too quick to try and be funny. Or they choreograph their set all at once and expand their brand before it's even good at the core. They don't work to be exceptional at their true talent first, and *then* stretch to tackle something else, then something else. There's no need to pressure yourself into doing something or being someone you're not. It's a *process*, and there's no need to expedite it for the wrong reasons or because you think you're behind."

Make Use of Your Time at the Bottom

With that attitude in mindset and heart, Andrew moved back home after college to the suburbs of Chicago. With no real delusions of grandeur at this point, he buckled down and was determined to learn. He didn't expect anything to really take off right away. He knew it would be a process. So for the first year and a half out of college, Andrew waited tables at a high-end chain of restaurants while he was getting his feet wet as a solo act.

"Those hours I spent playing at these restaurants were my music lessons. I was my own instructor learning and evolving and improving from my own experiences," Andrew says. "I practiced filling dead space between songs, controlling the dynamics of my voice, and putting on a show, not just singing songs back to back. And though these coffee shop and jazz club gigs were less than the attention we all want as artists, I knew it was critical for me to take the time to develop."

What most new artists forget is how essential that time at the bottom of the ladder is. That's the crucial time for an artist to discern who they are as a brand and an image, and find their niche, becoming comfortable in their artistic skin. If you're hell-bent on climbing that ladder unsure of who you are and lacking confidence, then there is a much higher chance of you falling flat on your face during the climb rather than ending up at the top.

After a couple years of maturing in his abilities to sing and put on a good show, Andrew found himself just floating without making any headway in his career because he was so tired and preoccupied with just life. Waiting tables is not easy, and he was working intense hours just to be able to support himself with the end goal of a music career. But the irony of the situation was that in all the work he was doing, he had no time or energy left to be creative. And this is ultimately where we see the majority of artists getting stuck. How do you make the transition? How do you get to the next level?

At the end of a particularly awful double shift one night, Andrew was faced with the cold, hard truth: *If I don't quit this mediocre job that is basically sucking all my time and energy, then I am never going to get anywhere.*

The prospect of letting go of the one outlet of financial support keeping him afloat to go chase this dream was terrifying, but he knew he never wanted to look back on his life and say he didn't give his dream everything he had. Even though he was getting some small traction around town and selling CDs each time he played, he knew that was an easy place to fool yourself, and he needed to step it up a notch. "The reality looked like I could very easily get stuck in this place," Andrew says. "So I decided not to wait for opportunity to knock, but to build a door instead."

It's amazing just how much you can accomplish and figure out how to get by when you have no other options. Necessity is a beautiful teacher. You have no choice but to be successful; your future depends on it. But not everyone is ready to be successful. You can believe you are, but there is a deliberate place where you learn to be coachable, yet stick to your values. You create opportunities and work until you are exhausted, but you don't confuse busyness with productivity. It's a place where you have deliberate goals written out, and even if you are the only one you can depend on, you will find a way to create value and get it done. That is where the *real* journey begins to a long and lucrative career.

Windy City Beginnings

After Andrew quit his job as a waiter, he moved straight to the heart of Chicago, seeking opportunity and a creative community to be a part of. There were quite a few pubs, bars, and restaurants that offered live music, so he started getting gigs there because of his well-crafted show. From there on out, it only got better.

The goal was to find a small booking agent who could increase his workload and get him into events, parties, and stuff like that to continue to build his name. His first agent was a small-time local guy he found through an acquaintance who came to one of his restaurant gigs. "I was talking about what I was looking for, and my friend said he thought he might know a guy who managed artists and helped book them jobs," Andrew says.

Close enough! He took the plunge and gave that agent a call. The guy could have been a nobody, but can you really not afford to make one more relationship? You never know what doors it can open. Andrew took the chance, and as it turned out, the agent quickly arranged an audition for him, where you play at a certain venue, then after your performance they either sign you on or not, depending on the feedback you get from them *and* the audience. The agent received wonderful feedback from the venue and signed Andrew on, booking him a few nights a week around town.

Marketing Strategy First, Then Record

Alongside playing more and more shows, Andrew kept developing new material and new music. After a few months after signing with the new agent and getting some good traction in Chicago, he decided it was time to record something better than those 10 songs he'd recorded in college.

He met a kid around town who was working out of the basement at his mom's house and was making great music. They ended up recording five songs, which became Andrew's first EP—"All Those Pretty Lights."

"The constant back and forth of ideas and experimentation that we did helped me gain a lot more confidence and go through the all-important development phase of discovering my own sound," Andrew says. "Having to compete with more and more layers of music, I was forced to discover that new side of my music, and I shifted from a soft and whispery musical tone to more mid-range and pop-rock. Recording my first real CD, it felt incredible! But like many artists, I didn't think about how to market it until it was done. Big mistake."

The only initiative they had planned toward marketing "All Those Pretty Lights" was buying one of those spam-bot things that sent out thousands of messages asking people to listen to his music on MySpace.

Nowadays, everyone is pretty much aware that these things are bots and not an actual person reaching out trying to start a genuine conversation. We definitely don't recommend them, but something that *is* pretty useful are social media productivity tools like SocialOomph, which help achieve the same goal. You can schedule tweets and Facebook status updates, integrate your blog and social media updates, automatically send direct messages in Twitter to new followers, and more. Direct messages are helpful for saying things like "Hey, thanks for following; hope you like our new video," with a link included to help drive traffic. Also, if you have somewhat of a following already, check out DemographicsPro for Twitter. It breaks down your followers into age, interests, what brands they like, what topics they talk about, etc. Knowing these analytics can make the difference between connecting with your fans or just being another tweet in their feed.

Twitter is an increasingly useful tool, especially when it comes to sales conversions, but there has to be a strategy. You have to make it *very evident* what you want people to do once they connect with you. No one is going to take the time to try to figure it out. And in the words of media mogul Gary Vaynerchuck, if you're not posting at least ten times a day on Twitter, you may as well not be on it. Whether or not you agree with that is up to you, but as far as anything related to online media and digital strategy goes, *consistency* is key. People have to know what to expect from you. That is the essence of what a brand is. Get your analytics from something like a DemographicsPro type of site to know who your demographic is, where they hang out, what they are talking about, and then *be* there. Join in the conversation—don't try to distract from it.

The Great Radio Experiment

Their social media marketing worked: After the release of "All Those Pretty Lights," Andrew was solicited on Twitter by a company in Minnesota that does college radio campaigns. They said that they liked his music and would love to do a campaign to help promote him as an artist. Not knowing what else to do to make his music known at the time, Andrew invested roughly $1,000 to try his hand at getting some traction in radio. Since it didn't look too professional to send a blank-faced CD with just his name on it, Andrew put together 300 small packages of pressed CDs, a photo, and a fact sheet about himself. In conjunction with the promotion team, they sent these CDs to program directors across the nation, trying to garner interest and radio play.

Essentially, these promotion companies solicit new business from independent artists. You pay them a fee in exchange for their radio relationships and contacts to send your mailers to. But when you're a brand-new artist and don't have momentum or many people talking about you, just mailing out a bunch of CDs and hoping one of them will strike a chord with the right person is a bit of a naïve approach and can be pretty fruitless. There's a lot of hope and a little bit of expectation when you try something new, and when things don't work out, it can be pretty devastating. Not to mention you can achieve the same result yourself and not pay someone $1,000 to do it for you.

"I guess I thought using the promotion company just looked more professional at the time. But today, I'm not sure I'd advise it. There was no actual strategy there; it was more of trying to throw something against the wall and see if it stuck," Andrew says. "I didn't plan any follow up or any personal contact with the program directors at each radio station. And sending a demo out without personal contact and thinking that they'll just put it in their playlist...well, it just doesn't work that way."

It's also the exact reason new artists with a budget, either self-funded or from a label, go on radio tours promoting their single and work their butt off to build *authentic* face-to-face relationships. But even the radio tour route is saturated and *very* expensive. At some point, you have to figure out which route you are going to hammer down on. Is it radio? Then get on a radio tour and line up shows along your route. Is it online? Get a marketing and sales funnel put together (Music Marketing Manifesto is great for this) and a plan for visibility. Is it touring? Get a budget and start calling venues! Where are you going to focus your efforts? You will see much better results focusing on primarily one or two main avenues and having a small presence in the rest.

Things Are Looking Up

Out of the 300 stations Andrew sent his demos to, hoping that they'd play his songs, only a few of them gave his music a couple of spins. While that did nothing to boost Andrew's confidence as an artist, there was one good thing that came out of those hundreds of CDs that he had sent.

That one good thing, which in retrospect might have been the trigger that got the ball rolling for his career, was the fact that he had unknowingly sent his demo to a music consultant who placed music in film, TV, advertising, and other media. Nic Harcourt, who was also the DJ for the highly influential music programs at LA-based public radio station KCRW, saw something special in Andrew's songs, played them, and decided he would use them in the *90210* remake. And the remake did very, very well.

"After the play on KCRW [and in the *90210* remake], I had gotten a few messages on MySpace, which were basically management offers, but nothing substantial ever became of most of them." But one message was from a guy in NYC named Seth Cassel, a marketing executive for Sony. When Seth reached out, Andrew was extremely skeptical. "It actually took me a few weeks to respond," admits Andrew, "but when I did, we got to know each other, and to this day he is still my manager."

Seth had the combination of persistence and patience that is so imperative for any budding artist. Andrew's gift is soulful, emotional, and meaningful music. Not every artist has a mind for marketing. Artists like Andrew, and most artists, in fact, need a little bit of guidance to maneuver through the industry. Seth was that guidance.

Right off the bat, Seth helped Andrew take steps in the right direction with his career. The fact that Andrew had already made a huge effort to get the ball rolling himself—releasing his first EP, getting the *90210* licensing deal, playing shows—just showed Seth that he was committed to doing this and willing to work. Seth was willing to add fuel to the fire.

Almost immediately, they decided it was time to get to work on another album. *The Ladder* became Andrew's first full-length album. The producer was a guy fresh out of music school who had an immense amount of talent but not enough experience to warrant the exuberant price most producers ask for. But with no funding to speak of, they needed a way to finance the project. (Seth may have had deep pockets as a Sony exec, but managers rarely fund an artist. They may help you find funding, but they typically will not fund you directly.)

"There were two things that Seth helped me accomplish immediately. He saw potential in sync and licensing [music placement] to film and TV because of the type of pop-rock music I played, and he decided to take advantage of it by approaching five or six nonexclusive licensing companies and giving them free rein with music placement," Andrew says. "Second, he came up with a formal business proposal to acquire funding for *The Ladder*."

Not everyone is fortunate enough to have an incredible family that is willing to put their money where their mouth is as far as their belief in you. When Andrew decided to ask his grandparents for help in creating this next album, he knew he needed to present his offer as a business plan and show them he was taking this project extremely seriously. Andrew and Seth presented Andrew's grandparents with a formal business proposal, complete with breakdowns of how they would use the funds to release the album, and ultimately, earn their money back.

It worked: His grandparents accepted the proposal. With their investment, they hired a publicist, producers, writers, and a whole slew of people who helped roll out the finished album. In the meantime, Andrew's music received a few more licensing opportunities, and because of that, they were able to pay back Andrew's grandparents almost within the same year.

In debt, and with little to no money in savings, Andrew was all in on this album. "With the budget we had, our strategy was to work with insanely talented people who hadn't just started out, but who also hadn't accomplished enough to charge a hefty rate—people like me," Andrew explained. "And people who genuinely liked our product and would work with complete passion."

The industry is about wins and losses, and the key is calculated risks. Write down a date six months from now and write what goals you are going to have accomplished by then. Then execute it like your life depends on it. These persistent, actionable steps are the keys to success. And to get it right, you must be fearless.

One successful and large enough licensing deal can lead to a domino effect that triggers more licensing opportunities. With Andrew's music being tailored to be perfect for soundtracks, he was able to take the opportunity and release new music fairly quickly afterward to keep up the momentum.

No one can tell you "this is what you should do, or this will 100 percent guaranteed work for you." No way. There's no carved-in stone path that leads to success; every musician is different, and every musician's definition of success is different too. Hopefully you want to enjoy the journey too.

Hanging 10

When Andrew had begun to get notoriety from his music placement and was seeing a steady, growing fan base, he was introduced to Ten Out of Tenn. Ten Out of Tenn. is a touring group of ten different singer-songwriters who come together to perform and support each other's songs in one massive show. The whole idea is to join arms and pool resources, talents, and audiences to play shows in a way that's beneficial and cost-effective to every artist involved.

Andrew discovered Ten Out of Tenn. while he was working on *The Ladder*. He needed a female vocal on a song, and he greatly admired the voice of Katie Herzig, an amazing singer-songwriter. He didn't know her personally, but he decided to reach out and see if she would sing on the track. Katie was coincidentally a part of Ten Out of Tenn. After explaining to Andrew about Ten Out of Tenn., she introduced him to the guys responsible for organizing the tour. Seeing Andrew's talent, they invited him to join the tour.

Connecting with your audience on a face-to-face level where you're raw and real is crucial for your success. To be known, you have to make people want to follow you, and digital media will only take you so far. Can you name any superstar who doesn't or didn't tour for years? It's that human connection that makes a true impact.

PRO TIP(S)

SUBMIT YOUR MUSIC FOR FILM/TV PLACEMENT

- *Submit to music placement sites like Music Xray, Rumble-fish, and Musicpage.* And there are plenty more you can find online. Have a presence on these sites, and make sure your profiles are complete. You never know who may find you or what opportunities will arise that you can apply for.

- *Try submitting to the several nonexclusive licensing companies online,* but make sure you only send your best. They are solicited every day, so make sure you stand out. And if you get presented with an agreement, have a well-qualified entertainment lawyer look over it.

- *Remember, your music must stand above the crowd.* The market is flooded. But there is a huge demand for amazing quality, hooky melodies, and music with emotion. However, it can't be cheap, thrown together, or lacking creativity if you want your music listened to and to be contacted.

You can always tell when someone is "green" by how comfortable they are with the microphone and the confidence they have. It takes getting used to, and it starts small. But building that skill is what ultimately leads to the opportunities for bigger and better stages. Even when you're just starting out and performing for five or ten people in a place where you've never set foot before, let alone played, you have to push through and do it anyway. Get comfortable.

If the opportunity comes, like it did for Andrew, and you aren't ready and experienced, it will pass you by.

"Going around in a massive tour bus and playing for an established audience gave me a glimpse into the life that I craved. It gave me a new perspective on the amount of effort that goes into having a career as big as that," Andrew says. "Touring with Ten Out of Tenn. benchmarked where I was at the time and allowed me to see just how much hard work would be needed to get to a similar point of success on my own."

Be Willing to Take a Chance

Around the time he was touring with Ten Out of Tenn., the MTV Breakout Artist of the Year award was running it's yearly contest. Seth, in his tenacity, forever unwilling to let an opportunity slide by, wanted Andrew to enter the competition. Andrew, as humble and modest as he is, was a little skeptical and told Seth it was probably pointless because there was no way he was going to win an MTV award.

Proof that your manager needs to be willing to believe in you as much as *you* believe in you, Seth was right. They entered the competition and to Andrew's astonishment, he made it into the top 10. The music, the art, the image...the package they had built for Andrew and all the hard work resonated and was paying off. Andrew made it from the top 10, to the top 5, and finally to the top 3. As a part of the top 3 contenders, Andrew had to play a show for 1,000 people in Chicago, and ultimately won the MTV award.

"The people who accomplish things are the ones that go for it," says Andrew. "I might not have been so willing to give this a shot in the beginning, but I put in my all once I did get behind it, and it paid off. You have to take hold of every single opportunity that comes your way, no matter how big or how small. You never know where it will lead. You just have to take your chances [and give] 100 percent until something changes or it doesn't work."

The music industry is one huge game of dominoes. One thing leads to another; you just have to be willing to take the first step and *keep going.*

There will never be a "sit back and relax because you made it" time, even for those at the top of the charts. They constantly have to keep surprising their audience and reinventing themselves and their product too.

Hello, Microsoft!

After Andrew won the MTV award, Microsoft came calling. They were coming out with a new phone in 2010, and they were doing a bunch of ad campaigns and commercials for the new Windows 7. One of the new directors had heard one of Andrew's songs on a short film that he had licensed a song to and he approached Andrew asking him to not only license his music for some of the campaigns, but to also write a custom song for it.

Andrew, who had never been the kind of a writer to actually come up with content just for commercial purposes, wasn't sure he was OK being told what to write. His lyrics tend to represent personal experiences or something at least conveying true emotion. Writing on demand would be a challenge.

Andrew agreed to custom write the song, but only under the specifications that he would have full creative control over how he crafted the song. Surprisingly, the director was pretty cool about it and let him run with it. "Admittedly, the song was a tad bit heavier than they wanted it to be, and I ended up shuffling around the lyrics somewhat for the Microsoft version," Andrew says. "Later, though,

I rereleased the original song on an EP, and in its essence 'Sky's Still Blue' is exactly the way I wanted my song to be."

How to Break into TV/Film Work

If you don't have a licensing agency you are working with to help get your songs placed in TV/film, you can do it on your own. Sites like those listed in our resources appendix are just a few of the services you can upload your music to, where music professionals are looking for music and songwriters for projects. And you don't have to wait for them to find you, you can answer the "want" ads on these sites if they fit your expertise.

You can even take it a step further and find music supervisor contacts online. Try running a search online to find what projects they are currently working on and see what's in their portfolio. Then you can send them an e-mail introduction and tell them that you see they are working on "X" project and you think you have a song that would be a good fit. Include a link to the song (attachments are not usually industry standard or welcomed, and often end up in spam) and a fact sheet about yourself.

If you get a placement, work that leverage to try and get more, which builds your resume and keeps the momentum going.

Success Is Not for the Faint of Heart

Leverage is what it's all about. In the early years, Seth and Andrew did most of everything themselves: talking to booking agents, advertising, distribution, running social media campaigns, and the rest. But as Andrew continues to grow increasingly more popular and constantly achieves new levels of success each year, they have leveraged that success into hiring publicists and specific people to keep his career moving forward alongside him so that Andrew can focus on doing what Andrew does best, creating music.

Going into the music industry, like with any career path, you've really got to assess yourself and see what sacrifices you're willing to make. Those sacrifices look like a lot of different things to different people. It could mean dropping out of school, selling the house, and traveling for months on end. Or it could mean finishing school, like Andrew did, and then setting off on a journey to explore all the various options that lay in front of you. Or it could mean something else entirely. This industry is a hard place to survive in, and if you have a plan B, by all means, keep it around, but if you don't, then don't look back.

There are more than a few sacrifices involved in making a living with your passion, because passion isn't always enough. You *start* with passion, but to beat out your millions of competitors for listening time, you have to add a ridiculously thick skin, an uncanny work ethic, sleepless nights, an incredible product, and outstanding marketing.

You *can* manifest success. But it usually comes in a way you aren't expecting. The bottom line is that a lot of the people who make a full-time living in the music business are those who just try insanely hard and don't give up when it gets even harder. Sometimes it's as simple as that.

What You See Is What You Get

To be successful as a singer/songwriter, you don't have to rely on gimmicks or drama to make a lasting impression. Anybody can write vague and generic songs, but it takes guts to write a song that stems from the very core of your being. Sincerity and honesty remain two values that Andrew tries to give to his fans. "My entire career and the success I have had as a musician and a songwriter are because I have never fed people made-up crock stories. That's not who I am or who I have ever been, and my fans don't expect that from me."

Andrew is a true representation of the artist mentality and putting in the time and dedication to his craft. Challenging himself to make each record better than the last and staying in front of his audience, there will be no shortage of success for Andrew Belle. We are proud to have him represent the cause that is How They Sell Music: artistry meeting ingenuity.

www.AndrewBelle.com

Facebook: Facebook.com/AndrewBelle

Twitter: @AndrewBelle

YouTube: YouTube.com/AndrewBelleMusic

Instagram: @AndrewBelle

CHAPTER FIVE

"The Road Dog"

CODY CANADA

How to Create a Platinum-Selling Career on Your Own Terms

> *Cross Canadian Ragweed legend and The Departed's front man, Cody shows artists how to create a career that spans decades by performing one concert at a time, night after night. His story is one of a true independent artist, who has built his career on his own terms—from subsisting on mustard sandwiches and playing local dives to eventually becoming the platinum-selling artist that every singer-songwriter dreams of.*

I'M JUST A TEXAS RESIDENT WITH AN OKLAHOMAN HEARTBEAT, AND I'M EXCITED TO tell you a little about myself and how I was able to create a career on the road, doing the one thing I'm most passionate about: music.

It's been 20-odd years since I first started making music, touring and traveling places. I plan on doing it another 20, and I don't think

I will get tired of it one bit. I was 4 years old when I attended my first concert: George Strait at a dinner theater in the '80s is where it all started, and I've had music in my soul ever since.

I picked up a guitar when I was barely 6 years old, just messing around with it. Few years down the road, I got myself a guitar book, a tuner, and countless discs and tapes of artists to listen to and learn from. The book taught me where to put my fingers on a guitar, and other artists, musicians, and their works taught me about tunes and melodies. That guitar spun me into a whole new world, and I was addicted to it. I spent every spare minute learning everything I could about playing music.

Even though I was born in Texas, I wouldn't necessarily say I was largely influenced by the Texas-style country or blues rock. I was 14 when I really started to focus on creating my own music and being the best I could at it. My career began with my friend Randy Ragsdale and myself playing at summer parties, just jamming out like teenagers do. Carting around a drum-kit in the back of his '85 Chevy truck, Randy and I would do acoustic sets at different places and just play together. People seemed to really enjoy it, but it wasn't taken that seriously. We were just playing live music because we loved to do it.

It was around this time that I took a trip to Stillwater, Oklahoma, for a concert and met Steve Littleton there. Steve introduced me to the guys in the country-music group The Great Divide, and I ended up joining the band in 1993. Things don't always work out, though, and I left the band just a few months later.

When I was leaving, the lead singer, Mike McClure, wanted to know what was next for me. I told him, "I'm going back home, starting a band, packing my stuff, and moving to Stillwater." And that's what I did.

That's when Randy and I got together and practiced songs in his living room, playing and writing music every night for three months straight.

Songwriter in Training

Before I met McClure and had that whole stint with The Great Divide, I was pretty naïve as far as songwriting, and didn't know much about the industry or how it worked. I had no idea there were people who just wrote songs and then the artists sang them. I thought that if I heard a George Strait song on the radio, George Strait must have written it. Artists have to wear so many hats, and not all artists are incredible songwriters. But there are incredible and beautiful songwriters out there who can't carry a tune in a bucket. So it was helpful to learn about co-writing with that mindset, and I have only grown as a writer by learning from some of the strongest up-and-coming writers in the business. McClure really opened me up to the whole songwriting process and learning to collaborate with others, not just writing by myself.

I learned how to write songs, slowly and gradually—and it was hard work. I know some people are just naturals, born with the ability to write a killer tune on the first go, but for others like myself, it takes a whole lot of practice. Here's the thing, though—a piece of advice for all the newbie singer-songwriters out there, and it is something I wish I'd realized from the start—when you're writing a song, just be honest and true to who you are and what you value. It's what makes you unique and a true artist, and it's what you have to share with the world. People are attracted to genuine artists, so learn the craft of songwriting and take the time to learn from others.

And don't chase the radio. If you are writing for what's on the radio right now, you are two years behind. While you may have to rewrite and correct and make changes, as you should with most songs, no one should write a song just for the heck of it and put out something mediocre as you're trying to grow a fan base. If your song doesn't mean anything to you, it won't mean anything to anyone else. Three incredible high-quality songs will always say more about you than 20 mediocre songs.

If you want people to connect with something you've put out, then do it the right way. Don't do a half-assed job of it—of anything really. Taking a shortcut and rushing a song, well—take it from someone who's been around for a while—it will fade out faster than the time it took you to write and record it. When I write a song, I toss it around, change it, study it, and play it at least 20 times before I'm comfortable with how it sounds.

Also, know your plan to release your single or record and have it planned out beforehand. I watch a lot of artists spend all this time and money recording, then the record is ready, and they just put it out with no real thought of how to promote it. Then they're surprised when it doesn't go anywhere. Most of the work happens before you even start recording the product.

A Shift in Genres and Attitude

From when I was a junior in high school and I started taking my music seriously, to the next four or five years, I sported a mullet and a cowboy hat, hitched rides, and played gigs here and there around Oklahoma and areas close by with my buddies after high school. My biggest musical inspirations were guys like George Strait and Merle Haggard. But during this time is when Nirvana and Pearl Jam hit it big, and my musical inspirations shifted big time.

The way these bands wrote music was incredible, like it was meant to be, raw and rugged, and that's what spoke to me. I loved the controlled chaos of their sound; the roughness of it was awesome to me ...so much so that I hung up the cowboy hat, cut my hair, and bought myself some Doc Martins. I was midway between a country singer and a rock singer.

We formed the band Cross Canadian Ragweed in 1994, and we were pretty much doing the same thing for a few years; playing small gigs, events, bars, clubs, but we weren't really going anywhere in terms

PRO TIPS

BOOK YOUR OWN TOUR

- *Make the commitment.* You've got to know this is a process and commit to making sacrifices, traveling, and living unglamorously for quite a while. Once that decision is made, you begin to build relationships with club owners one step at a time.

- *Reach out to venues yourself or have someone act as your agent, even if it's your wife or a friend.* Have an amazing press kit with all the information they need to be able to promote you. Put yourself in their shoes and think about why they would be inclined to book you. How are you going to make them money?

- *Start regionally and build that local following; they will become your die-hard fans.* It works much better than traveling all over the country, losing money, and not building momentum with a certain audience. Start in a region, nail it, and make sure you are growing the audience every single time. After a while, you will know when you are ready to expand, travel longer distances, and make it worthwhile financially.

of business. I loved and focused too much on the music to pay attention to the business side of things. If you had asked someone else, they'd say we were stuck in a rut.

Musically, things were great, but if we were going to do this seriously, for a career, then we needed to get our stuff out there to the masses. Playing in dives and clubs wasn't going to get us anywhere.

Shannon to the Rescue

This is where my wife comes in. Meeting her in Stillwater was probably the best thing that ever happened to me and my music.

As I said, we'd been at this a while, and yet we weren't really going anywhere. Shannon was quick to point that out to me. While I thought that that was pretty much the way things worked in the music industry, she disagreed and wanted to pitch in and do what she could to help us.

We had a rough-cut demo that we called "The Turquoise Tape". It was mostly covers and had maybe one original song on it. We didn't really do anything with it, but she said let's make a CD. So that's what we did.

Shannon dived into the whole thing and really took us on. She went to South by Southwest and attended Sharon Osbourne's (Shannon's hero) seminar/interview about how she championed Ozzy through the years. Some of the key takeaways: let the artist be who they are and market them to the venues, sponsors, and festivals that fit; keep your wife and manager roles separate; and do not discuss money. Shannon got most of her inspiration and drive from Sharon's seminar, and it gave us the kick in the ass we needed to take our shows up a notch.

We started pitching to radio—college radio mostly, because we were that age and we connected with that demographic. While none of us planned to go to college ourselves—two of us didn't even graduate high school—we knew our sound appealed to college kids, so that's where we focused our attention. We started playing at bars with people our age, and we were well received.

Pitching to college radio was decently easy in Stillwater. We knew the area, we knew the people, and because we were around so much—playing gigs at every other place—people knew us too. We would open for country artist Pat Green when he came through, and we would rock the place. It would be overflowing.

Ragweed didn't plan on reaching for Nashville or any of those places; that wasn't our goal. I had friends who'd had record deals in Nashville, and it wasn't all it's made out to be. We decided to go the grassroots route, and though we knew it would take twice as long, we thought it was the way we were meant to go.

To be successful in anything in life, you have to be genuine and make connections; doesn't much matter if you're a rock star or a businessman. If people like you, they'll make the effort to help you, promote you, or support you. I've seen people pay DJs thousands of dollars to get radio play, and the radio guy would take their money but only give them a couple spins. I always preferred sitting down with them, chatting over a beer or two, and being actual buddies. That approach has served us very well, even though it's more of a process. These people will support us forever; we didn't try to buy our way in. When you build genuine fans and friends, you have that relationship and foundation to back it up. When you sign to a label off the bat or spend a bunch of money to get fast notoriety, when/if things go wrong, you lose everything because you didn't have an established fan base that knew you and has grown with you. If you have that fan base, you have the control and the key to drive your career. No label, management, or publishing company can take that from you.

When we were on the road, getting on the radio was easy. We would call the station before we came to town, let them know we were playing a local venue, and we wanted to swing by, say hello, and chat. Simple as that, and the best way to do it as you are getting started. They appreciated our approach, and our genuine reputation started to build on itself.

I've made so many friends in the music industry operating this way, and making a connection is the etiquette for pitching to radio—if there is one. That's how we progressed in anything: We made friends with our fans and with people in the industry.

Create Your Own Sound

Ragweed sounded the way it did for a number of reasons. We just went with the flow. We never did anything fancy to make ourselves sound different. Ragweed was a band with the basics: a guitar, a rhythm guitar, bass, and drums. In fact, we named one of our records "Garage" because that is essentially what we were.

If you're trying to find your sound and a way into the industry, don't try too hard. Things don't turn out the way you want them to if you try to force them. You end up sounding like your influences, and that's where people find connections and make comparisons for the most part. For example, at the beginning of Ragweed, there were tunes I was writing that had a sound similar to that of Mike McClure. But that's because he was the one mentoring, teaching, and training me. Our sound of music, what people most associate us with even now, with The Departed, is a product of pure accident and just the evolution of my career.

Don't set out to try and emulate someone's technique and composition. Be inspired by others, learn from them, but never try to exactly copy them. You will never be the artist you admire, and no one will ever be like you. You are unique and individual in your own right; you don't need to be someone else to succeed.

Don't Give Into Setbacks

At the beginning, when you're starting out, I think it's so important to not give up too soon or get jaded by setbacks. It takes a long time to build momentum to propel you to where you want to be. There are going to be times when you're paid crumbs, opening for somebody that isn't doing much better than you are, but you've got to push through and learn from every opportunity.

For example, we went to Lubbock six times—and it was terrible! The crowd didn't like us much, and yet we kept going back. Lubbock being such a football town was not something we cared about. So our last show there I yelled out from the stage, figuring I had nothing to lose in this town: "Hey, we are here to play music for you people, and we don't give a crap about football. We are here for you to have a good time and drink some beer!" Somehow that got people's attention, and everyone came over to the stage. Building a career on the road is 100 percent about persistence.

The first time we went to Illinois, we put on a show and played for 20 people. The next time we went, we played for 50, and the time after that, we played for 100 people. They didn't have a lot of music like ours up there. We had a show worth talking about and people would bring their friends the next time we came to town.

We took the time after the shows to bond with the people who came. No egos involved. This is the way it builds. Fame doesn't happen overnight, and you don't get hordes of people running after you after one performance. It's a long, and sometimes painful, process. But if music is who you are, not just something you want to do, it's worth it.

Working to make it in the music industry is tough as hell. If you're a regular Joe, like we are, you won't have managers to look after you, flipping the place upside down at your every beck and call. We all had jobs to support us and make ends meet to start. We'd have day jobs along with our night gigs. My wife, Shannon, worked at a software company during the day and bartended at night.

Since we were on the road so much, most of our money would go into keeping/maintaining our conversion van. All our gigs were tip-jar gigs, where we'd make a couple hundred bucks at most and rely on merchandise sales. We had a good friend who ran a printing shop draw up some bad-ass t-shirt designs. So for shows when we weren't really making anything on the booking fee, our t-shirt sales would usually pay out more than the show! Our merchandise sales kept us alive for several years. Never underestimate the power of a great design, and don't skimp on your merchandise in the early stages. It will be the majority of your revenue to start, and it increases awareness of your band. Our merchandise was a huge reason we were able to stay on the road touring.

Speaking of which, no matter how small the take, we all split the pot evenly at the end of the night. The front man, or whoever, doesn't get more than everyone else. That is still just as important to me today. We are a band and we are team and like-minded in everything we do, or we just don't do it.

Sometimes You Have to Improvise

To book shows, we used Shannon as our "booking agent." She would use her maiden name when calling to book us. If she called clubs saying that "her husband's band was awesome!" as you can imagine, that wouldn't get us very far.

She would call a venue of similar size to the ones we were selling out and say she was the booking agent for Cross Canadian Ragweed, then tell them we were selling out the Wormy Dog Saloon at "X" capacity. Since most of the people in that market were college kids in Oklahoma, if we would call Blue Rose in Tulsa, we knew our crowd of kids would follow and we could get at least 65 people through the door, or whatever it was. Anything we could do to lessen the risk on the club we would do, as we still needed to prove ourselves. We just wanted to play! So if Blue Rose offered us $250 to come do a show, we would usually take it.

We would just keep going back to each market, and our crowd got bigger each time. We hung out with the fans before shows and after shows, and they really felt a part of our growth and were the biggest contributors to it. They followed us because we made it feel like we were all in it together; we had no egos, we just loved playing music and putting on a great show.

Rock or Perish?

Honestly, my advice for those who want to do this for a living is be prepared because this isn't something your mother would be very happy with; you need to quit your jobs if you really want to do this and get to the next level. It's not going to be a smooth sail. But you have to go all in and figure out how to make ends meet if you want to build your career on the road. You can't hold a stable job with the demands of running a tour. In our marriage vows, Shannon and I said we were all in, even if it meant living on mustard sandwiches (which we did for quite a while!), and that deep dedication and focus is what has seen us through.

As things started to pick up, and our gigs started to get farther away, there came a point where it was next to impossible to make it back to work on time the next morning. So in 2001, we all quit our jobs to focus on music full time.

If you're dedicated to music and want to start building your life on the road, you will have to make a decision: Are you willing to play gigs, go all out, and survive on mustard sandwiches, every day for a while? I reached that decision when I got into a really bad wreck. I almost died, and that's the day I told my wife that I was done working and ready for music to be present in my life, all day, every day. Nothing made me happier than being on the road, having the time of my life.

I can't say the decision I made was an easy one or even a sensible one, but it was a decision I was content with. Without a stable job to support you, it's tough. It's tougher still for the family that sticks by you. And while those may have been the most difficult times of our lives, I have never regretted taking that step.

It's a gamble. Sure it may never work out, or you might be not as successful as you would want, but knowing that you never tried, never gave it a shot, is much harder to live with than being satisfied with the thought that you did your best.

Keep On Pushing

For the next few years all Ragweed did was travel and play music, and connect with our fans. We were making so much noise around the Texas/Oklahoma area that people were beginning to really notice us. We didn't go crazy pushing for a label deal because that's not who we are and not what we represent. We just played music because that's what we cared about.

We organized all our gigs ourselves: Coordinating and matching dates, venues, locations, merchandise, and whatever else; we did everything. If there was a major act coming to town, like Willie Nelson, and we wanted to open for him, Shannon would call the booking agent and ask to open. She would tell them who we were, what our local draw was, and what we could contribute. We would do whatever it took to get the slot.

It's so important to build a great reputation when you are the opening act, especially for a national act. You should be insanely respectful of their time, and don't make it about you. Don't overplay your set, and don't hound the main act, asking for autographs and all that. Make a great impression, and next time someone comes through, the booking agent knows you are a great bet, bring a great crowd, and aren't a hassle. That helped us a lot. Shannon got us so many bookings just by her amazing etiquette and natural brain for the business. She really was the fifth member of the band. Right from when I met her, until today, all she's ever told me is to just focus on the music and she'll take care of the rest. And she really has. If you're familiar with Ragweed or The Departed's work and our songs, you'll know exactly how big a part she's been in our lives. I've got multiple songs written and recorded that are dedicated to her.

Shannon by my side was a source of constant reassurance for me. She lifted me up when there were times where things wouldn't be looking too good for Ragweed. We'd made our presence known sufficiently around Texas that we were playing shows for thousands of people at a time, and yet, outside that little bubble, no one had hardly heard of us, let alone known us musically. For example, we played a gig for 24,000 one night in Texas, and we went to Michigan for our next show where nobody knew us at all. There were like 30 people there! As I said earlier, you've got to scale your business one region at a time and just keep going back.

Keeping the Indie Spirit—Label or Not

We had three records out, all on our independent label, Underground Sound, and we'd made ourselves prominent enough around the region that the big labels came calling. They did so largely because of our sales. The venues have to report their numbers to various outlets, Pollstar and whatnot, and our name kept showing up. For an independent act, they were consistently pretty high. So we were on the radar, and eventually, the labels got a hold of us when they saw we were consistent and not going anywhere.

Label reps would come to watch us play live, and that was when things really took off. We were a touring band and played enough live that we put on a great show, so they were impressed.

As I said earlier, we weren't really interested in Nashville-style record deals where the label just takes over. While these people saw that we were making money and they saw profitability and they wanted a cut, we had been so used to working things how we did them that their way wasn't going to fly with us.

We didn't want to be superstars and focus on the monetary benefits while forgetting and leaving behind our passion for making music and playing for our fans. What we wanted was just to be able to continue to provide our extremely loyal fans with an experience that they'd remember for a long time. That was something we were not going to compromise on.

When labels started coming after us, we met with a few of them to see what it was all about and decided that Universal South offered us a good platform to maintain the lifestyle we wanted. We signed a six-record deal, and they wanted to redo and release our previous album. We weren't in favor of that, and instead, we wrote and recorded a new one. The "Purple" album, released in 2007, was our first with a major record label.

We had leverage going into the deal since they came to us, so we were able to structure it so the label didn't make any money from all the touring we did. Normally, in a recording contract, they give you "X" amount for a bus, a tour manager, and all that. We were already a touring act, so we didn't need all that. Besides, we knew it was just a loan, so we didn't take any money from them and they didn't make any from our shows. It was strictly a record deal. We even paid for recording our own albums. We would get it done by their deadlines, and they would promote it and make their money that way. When we went on the road, we bought our albums at wholesale from the label and sold them at retail and kept the cash. We did have to recoup the promotional dollars they spent to advertise the record, though, but that was OK. They promoted our band, and we got a bigger platform for it. Seems crazy, but we just took as little money as possible from the label.

Retaining the "indie band" mentality and image has always been really important to us; we have never wanted to sell out for the corporate "look." That's not who we were. Even when the label wanted to buy certain ads at a radio station that didn't want to play us, to hopefully coerce them *to* play us, we fought them over it. If they weren't playing us organically because they liked our music, then we didn't want to pay them to play us. I would much rather be written up in *American Songwriter* than *pay* to get a write-up in *Billboard*. I wanted us to *earn* the write-up in *Billboard*.

Be Loyal to Your Fans

The reason why we, Ragweed and now The Departed, have such diehard fans is for a few reasons, but, ultimately, I would say it's because they are loyal to us, and we're loyal back. I don't believe in sitting at the merchandise table, with all the things that we're selling laid out between us, having a chat with fans after the show. That's like sending subliminal messages that say, 'Hi, we're here and we'll talk to you but only if you're buying some of our stuff.'" That's not being a true artist, that's being desperate.

I'd much rather grab a beer or three at a local bar and have real conversations and get to know our fans. They're real people; they support you and pay attention to you, and spend their hard-earned money on you. They're the reason for your bread and butter, so show them the respect and attention that they deserve. Be friends with your fans, and be good to each other. Be nice to people and get to know their story. We have so many fans who we can call family just because of the connection. Fans don't forget that individual face time and that you went above and beyond to get to know them. Most bands don't.

The End of an Era

Universal South understood that and was really passionate about our work. Tony Brown and Tim DuBois, the heads of the label at the time, really connected with our music, and the three years working with them were fabulous. Things started to go south when these guys parted ways with the label and some new guys took over. Our champions were gone, and the other guys hadn't grown with us and didn't have the same passion for us. I can't even say for sure if they ever listened to any of our stuff or cared about it at all.

When you find yourself stuck in any situation where you feel like the other person—manager, label head, or anyone else—may not have your best interests at heart, leave. To maintain our integrity, we had to. We were fearful of getting shelved because they didn't have the passion for us the way Tony and Tim did. However tough it may be, you deserve someone who will 100 percent back you and be truly involved and passionate about what you're doing. It's better to have it in control than have the false security of what a record label can provide.

We fulfilled five of the six records we had contracted for. After that, fortunately or unfortunately, Ragweed had a hard time handling the loss of stability, and a few of the guys decided to part ways.

Given the fact that we weren't really happy with our label, tensions were rising all over, affecting everyone, including my wife and me; we weren't on the best terms. Unfortunately, you get one bad attitude or something like that on the road, where you're in such close proximity with others, and it just spreads. Slowly and steadily, we started getting bigger holes in our boat.

The breaking point happened at a gig in Stillwater: Someone threw a bottle on stage, cracked open my head, and knocked me out, and things sort of blew up. Everything got out of hand, and that's when Ragweed decided we were officially done as a band.

As scary and nerve-wracking as those days were, you have to realize you can't let something like a break up of a band, even one you've been with for 16 years, stop you from doing what you love. Not all relationships are meant to last, and if you are built to do this, it's in your DNA and you have to find a way to keep going.

I was panicky, sick to my stomach, and troubled about it. After all, it was the end of an era. I'd been doing this a long time, and now suddenly I was kind of hung in the middle without any direction. You just figure out how to move past what life gives you. You're going to have battles in your career, and you have to be ready for that. When Ragweed was coming to an end, I knew I was still going to be playing music; there was never any question about that. But what I wasn't sure of was how the hell you start over again.

A Fresh Start

Jeremy Plato, our bass player, and I met for a beer and decided that as scary as the whole thing might be, we were sticking together and starting a new band. That's what we had to do. We just had to take a deep breath and begin somewhere.

When Jeremy and I decided to start The Departed, we still had around 20 to 30 gigs booked for Ragweed. We began practicing The Departed in between the gigs that Ragweed decided we were still going to fulfill.

Going in that new direction, I knew we'd probably lose about half our fans, and we did. With the transition, a lot of our fans were mad. They felt a personal connection with Ragweed and automatically weren't going to be on board with The Departed.

It was a different sound, and there were going to be people who weren't going to be comfortable with that. It wasn't something that was very easy to accept, but we couldn't back down. It's been a difficult transition, even almost four years down the line. But now I think we're on the right track, and we're comfortable in our new skin. We have let it grow organically as we always have.

For artists, our music evolves and changes as we do. Because much of our inspiration comes from our everyday lives—or for me it does—as we grow and evolve, it's reflected in our work. Your life might be walking an entirely new path with each record as compared to your last. And sometimes, fans will have a hard time adjusting to that change. You just have to do your thing, though, and let it make you happy and fulfilled.

The toughest part of being in a situation like mine, where you end one thing only to begin another, is rebranding. You are the same person and some people will only ever associate you with your past act. To get them to acknowledge the newer aspect is quite difficult.

Perseverance, the reoccurring theme song of the music industry, will get you through anything. We made a decision that we were all equals, and the band was either going to be great together or be crappy together.

You will end up somewhere, even if it was not where you intended. And most of the time it's not. You can't make it out unscathed, but believe me, if you honestly want to, you will survive this and a whole lot more that life throws you.

With The Departed, we decided the best thing to do to put ourselves and our new band out there was to release a record. I thought there wasn't a better time to fulfil the promise I'd made myself, to release an album of covers of all the great songs written by my fellow Oklahomans. To record and release "This Is Indian Land" probably wasn't the best decision in hindsight because it confused our fans, but hey, some people dug it, and I learned from it and crossed it off my bucket list. You can't expect to know how it's going to go, really. It's a learning process. Sometimes you're going to get it right, sometimes not so much.

Build the Career You *Want*

I understand it's a little different for the artists who want to break through the Nashville way. This whole being on the road, self-releasing records kind-of gig isn't for everyone, but that's who we are and who I've always been as an artist. It just goes to show that there are other ways to get your talent and music to the masses, create a career on your own terms, and get it known other than pounding down record-label doors and waiting for someone to open up and give you a chance. You can create your own opportunity if you want it bad enough.

Beating the streets is how we do it and how many artists do it. There are a number of ways you can build your fan base without pouring money into someone else's pockets, especially money that you may not have at the start. Pour every penny back into developing yourself, and take one day and one show at a time.

You can be consistent and make a name for yourself at one place and then branch out, like I did. I played an acoustic show at one bar for three whole years before I moved elsewhere. You can become a nomad and move from place to place and travel and make friends along the way. That's how Ragweed did it in the beginning. Back then social media wasn't a big deal, and to be honest, I'm not that well-versed in the Internet ways today, but I do know it's a platform you can really use to your advantage. However, if it's not something you feel passionate about, I wouldn't focus on it too much. I'd focus on what you do best and do that incredibly well.

I really think that social media acts like a prelude to that face-to-face connection that I so believe in. The few times I've used any of the social media networks, it was mostly to chat with the locals of the place I'm visiting next: ask them the best place to eat or have a drink and people reply. They interact and appreciate that one-on-one and taking the time to get to know the town I'm passing through.

Everything circles back to the people, the fans. That's what will give you a career. Fans that you connect with are the ones with the power to make or break you. Give them the respect they deserve because ultimately that's who puts a roof over your head.

I like being independent when it comes to my music because I'm my own boss. I don't have people telling me what to do, what song to write, or what not to sing. Being on your own gives you the creative freedom that some of the signed artists never have.

It's ten times harder to get yourself known on your own than it is through the labels, I'll admit that. They have a whole army and arsenal that you don't, but they also have all the control. As The Departed, when we were leading up to the release of our second album, "Adventūs," to bring awareness to the fans, my wife came up with the idea to release a new song every Monday for free until the full album came out. Something like this probably wouldn't sit right with a traditional label. We were basically giving our music away, and yet, just because we had the special, close connection with our fans, when we asked them to buy the complete album regardless of already having the pre-released songs, some way or the other, they did!

While I personally am all for giving away music for free, I understand that's not something that most artists—and definitely not most labels—will be comfortable with. But if you're actively building a fan base, this is one of the best ways to do so in the beginning in my opinion. If people haven't heard of you before and no one is raving about you, there's not a super strong chance anyone is going to risk money buying an album they have no idea if they will like.

If your music is just out there, available free, and people like it, they will share it, which is exactly what you want. Word-of-mouth advertising is the best you can get, so make it extremely easy for people to get a hold of what you want them to.

Ultimately, you can build the career you want. I did it on the road, and I'll be a lifer.

I hope my story has been of some help and an encouragement to stay true to exactly who you are as an artist. The confidence sells itself.

See you on the road,

WE HANG OUT HERE

www.thedepartedmusic.com

Facebook: Facebook.com/shancanmusic

Twitter: @departed_music

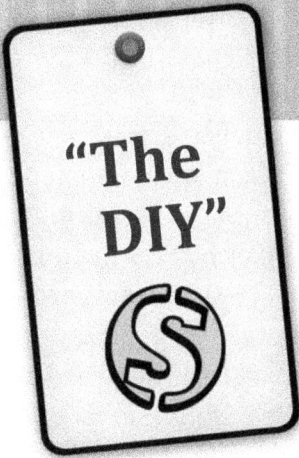

CHAPTER SIX

"The DIY"

MR. BILLY

Marketing 101: Build a Rock-Solid Career at Any Age, in Any Genre

> *Mr. Billy is a classic rock music lover, dad, and marketing genius turned full-time, six-figure artist. With twenty-eight albums and counting—and no major label to back him—Mr. Billy demonstrates that anyone with enough desire and work ethic can make a career in the music industry. #mindblown.*

MY NAME IS WILLIAM CHARLES GRISACK III, BUT YOU CAN CALL ME BILLY. MY STORY may be a little different than most folks who make a living making music. As of writing this, I've been in the music business full time since 1979—that's thirty-five years.

As a child, the music business was the only business I knew where you could make money. Now before you write me off as an out-of-touch wacko, let me tell you a little about my family and upbringing.

I was born in 1961. My parents were part of a family musical entertainment business. My grandfather, Bill Sr., was a local big band leader in Philadelphia. My dad, Bill Jr., was a semi-famous jazz musician who worked with giants like Dizzy Gillespie and Stan Kenton, and did arrangements for Rosemary Clooney. My mom was a professional lounge singer. My grandmom, aunts, and uncles all played music as a hobby, too. So as you can see, from an early age I had a different world view of the potential of music as a full-time career. In my family, it was understood that you would follow in the footsteps of your parents and grandparents. Getting a day job was sort of frowned on—something you did as a last resort when gigs were hard to come by.

My grandfather taught me how to be a showman, how to entertain and schmooze with the crowd, how to give them what they want—and more. My dad showed me the importance of being a monster musician, really knowing your shit, how to improvise, and how to play with passion. My mom was a master at sales, manipulating buyers and getting paid top dollar. Other relatives helped me understand the joy of making and listening to music.

What exactly have I done with this family musical education?

- Played music professionally (aka getting paid) for the last thirty-five years

- Still play gigs every week, averaging 150 to 250 paying shows a year

- Played professionally in forty-nine states (anyone have a gig in Hawaii for me?), Canada, Newfoundland, and Greenland

- Performed on U.S. Department of Defense tours

- Written, recorded, and released hundreds of songs

- Released three vinyl 45s, many digital singles, and twenty-eight albums in a variety of styles

- Won many awards including iMedia and CMW

- Repeatedly voted best family entertainer in Wisconsin

- Opened for or worked with many big-name acts

- Featured on radio, print media, and blogs

- Appeared on many TV shows as a musical guest or interviewed as a newsmaker

- Written, recorded, and released twelve full-length CDs in just twelve months

- Host a podcast with guerrilla music marketing pioneer and author Bob Baker

- Supported my family; bought cars, homes, and all the necessities of life as an independent musical entrepreneur

- Worked as a booking agent for bands

- Taught guitar and bass

- Own independent record label

- Made my fair share of mistakes

Let's not forget the have-nots. I have not:

- Won a Grammy (yet)

- Been signed to a major label deal

- Ever been considered a thin, good-looking guy with a great voice

Who Is This Guy?

You're probably wondering: Who the hell is this guy? How is this possible? How can I do the same thing?

From the time I was twelve to about sixteen, I played guitar in a band with my mom (vocals/drums), dad (drums/sax), and grandfather (bass). We did mostly jazz standards and pop songs of the day. I basically hated it; I wanted to play "Smoke on the Water" not "The Girl from Ipanema." But people loved us—my grandpop was a showman, my dad had chops, and my mom added the classy sex appeal. I, of course, was the token rock star! We always attracted lots of tip money and got booked with a big fat raise. But I wasn't happy.

When I was sixteen I quit the band, quit school, and left my family to be a rock star. I jumped in the garage with some friends, started writing songs we liked, and created a sound that was *cool*. We didn't get one damn gig. So there I was, homeless and broke. I was at a crossroads that would define my music career forever—making moneymaking music that people wanted to hear, or making music I wanted to hear and not making much money. At the time, I thought this was the difference between playing covers and originals. I was wrong, but I'll explain later.

At least I had the sense to realize I needed money. So began my full-time music career. I went from band to band, style to style, playing guitar, bass, drums, keyboards, fiddle—anything that would keep me employed. I eventually realized that the lead singer or bandleader was making the most money and getting the most attention, two things I desperately wanted. I soon made the transition to bandleader, lead singer (even though I sucked at singing), and wild, comedy-infused front man—a role that saved my ass. (A great front man is worth ten times more than a great singer any day of the week!) I started creating set lists based on songs and music styles that most people (who went out to hear live music) wanted to hear. But I still wasn't satisfied.

From a very early age, lip-syncing to Beatles songs in front of my bedroom mirror, I wanted to be a rock star; the kind of celebrity that people came to see, on purpose. I wanted people to come hear my original music, not some covers to get drunk to and chase girls (or guys) at the bar. I'd already spent the '70s and '80s playing covers of other people's music. I was done.

Give the People What They Want

It was the 1990s. Grunge opened the door to the indie movement, and I started writing and recording again. At first I started writing the same old shit everyone else does—self-centered, noncommercial stuff that didn't sound anything like my live show. That was when I had my first real epiphany about selling music.

I had become really good at marketing my band, getting gigs, and getting paid more than bands that were way better than my groups were. The secret was giving the people what they wanted. I was a funny and high-energy front man. I was also 5 foot 5 and 300 pounds with bad hair. To get booked and booked back, I surrounded myself with rock gods—skinny, good-looking dudes who could sing, and who also had chick appeal, cool moves, and great hair. I eventually perfected this idea and created Billy Zack and the Attack. In the Midwest, where classic rock was still king, we had a hit in the early '90s called "Dropkick the Bitch." This band became a music and merchandise marketing machine.

We had it all; the band looked and sounded great. We played four to six nights a week. The party girls loved the rock boys in the band. The guys who came to the shows loved real rock music and wanted to go where all the girls went. We released our first CD, called "Booby Trap," which was nothing but songs about members of the opposite sex we knew. The naming of the CD, the cover, and the inside artwork were exercises in marketing genius designed to make you want to buy two copies at a time.

I was way ahead of the times, as this CD was crowd-funded twenty years before Kickstarter or any of the other crowd-funding sites. Before we started thinking of recording, a fan gave me $20 at a gig and asked me to send her a copy of our first CD when we made one. The rest of the week I started telling everyone we were making a CD and to give me $20 for limited edition signed and numbered copies. And they did! I raised enough to buy the equipment to record our first CD and release it, in sixty days.

We sold thousands of CDs ("Booby Trap" and "Big Dreams") and countless hats and t-shirts. Selling band merch in large quantities requires a strategy. You can't just put up a merch table and watch the stuff fly off the shelves. For Billy Zack, it was about the theme. We had a brand, a hot song, and a slogan. Everything we sold revolved around that. But here is what we did that pushed us *way* over the sales cliff. I realized that more guys bought hats and shirts, so we hired really cute and sexy girls to walk around the venues wearing our hats and shirts. They went from table to table, person to person, selling our merch and music, and signing up folks on our mailing list. The girls worked for commission, so they were very motivated to sell, and they had some great marketing ideas of their own, including wearing several shirts and letting buyers remove them, or putting the shirts and hat on the buyers themselves. We had to order more stock every week.

The band lasted about ten years, until I finally had to retire due to health issues. I was able, however, to resist getting a day job by offering my services as a website designer and Internet marketer (things I learned to do running the band) for other businesses. I made a very nice living doing this until I was able to return to music with even more success than I had ever known. I was playing all originals, getting paid more than ever, doing TV shows, and winning awards. And it didn't look anything like I'd imagined it would.

PRO TIPS

MARKET TO YOUR TARGET AUDIENCE

- *If you plan to make money and actually sell your music, never ever release anything your target market wouldn't be interested in.* For instance, if you are a comedy type of artist *do not* release serious stuff. If you're not political, don't go there either.

- *Always know how your ideal fan listens to music.* If they don't buy CDs, maybe you don't need to make CDs. Do they stream? Download? Buy vinyl? Do some research and find the easiest way to get in front of them.

- *Artwork and colors are very important.* Most music album and singles artwork online is only seen slightly larger than a postage stamp. Don't put your face on the cover unless your face is well known. Use that space to put something appealing to your target fan. In my genre bright colors, cartoons, and animals sell CDs. What turns on your crowd? T&A? Psychedelic images? Motorcycles? Beer? Religious images?

- *Always make it easy for people to find you the way they want to find you.* If you hate Facebook or Twitter, get over it.

- *Make is super simple for buyers to pay any way they want to.* Period.

The Creation of Mr. Billy

Enter "The Mighty Mr. Billy," my current full-time musical career.

Ever seen the movie *Happy Gilmore* with Adam Sandler? It's the story of a hockey player who isn't very good, but he ends up being this freak-of-nature golfer. All he wanted to do was be a pro hockey player but his skill set (super slap shot), matched with a lucky break, equaled a pro golf career. Something similar happened to me. I wanted nothing more than to play original music to a captive audience that came to see me. Period. And that is what I got; I just didn't know that my fans would be 3-feet tall.

In 2001, I was a middle-aged guy with a wife, house, and two kids. I'd been off stage for about a year and a half, and I thought any chance I had to have a "real" music career was over. My five-year-old son (who, ironically, is now the full-time drummer in my band) asked me to be his "show and tell" for kindergarten class. I brought a guitar to show the kids, and the teacher asked me to play some songs for them, which was fine, but I didn't know any kids' songs! I did some classic rock songs and the kids and teachers loved it; one even said I should do this for a living. I thought, at the very least, this might be a fun hobby.

Feeling energized after the fun I had, I did some research and found out that, at the time, there were no rock acts for children, just folk singers. I decided that would be my USP (unique selling point). I already knew that people in the Midwest loved classic rock, so I figured the kids would too. I joined the Children's Music Network, an organization made up of musicians, songwriters, and educators who work with children. I built a website, picked up the phone, and started calling schools and libraries looking for gigs.

I used all the tricks I learned from my rock band days and applied them to my new career. I knew I had to make money fast since this was now my full-time job...again. So I decided to use the media to market my new creation. I booked myself on all the local TV morning and noon shows as a musical guest. In smaller markets, this isn't too hard to do. There are always morning shows, noon shows, and other talk and variety opportunities available, especially if you find a way to make yourself "newsworthy" in some way.

If you are thinking of getting booked on a TV morning or noon show, first you need to know if the program books musical performers. If they do, are they smaller acoustic acts or full-blown bands? Do the musical guests just perform, or is there a talking or interview segment? Do your research.

Next, find out who the talent or guest coordinator or producer is. This type of information is usually easy to find on the station website or by asking the receptionist. I like using the phone as a first contact, but email works too. Just keep inquiries short and to the point. Do not bug media contacts!

I started finding events and other newsworthy reasons for local newspapers to write about me. I tried to get a slot at any event, paid or not, that had a built-in audience ready for what I had to sell. For about two years, I hit it hard and I was everywhere. Desperation will do that to you. I knew that if I didn't succeed I wouldn't be able to pay the bills.

I looked for opportunities and found them everywhere. I read every entertainment publication and joined every local band and solo artist mailing list that did anything remotely similar to what I did. I checked out direct and indirect competitors' websites on a regular basis. I tried to find the holes that other acts were missing, or just didn't want to do. I landed regular weekly gigs at a few local malls, children's museums, and family-friendly businesses that never had live music before. I truly believe there is no shortage of opportunities; there is only a shortage of people who notice them and take advantage of them.

I stacked the deck in my favor by writing songs using the most popular topics of interest to kids and recording them in a 1980s classic rock style that parents loved. I crowdfunded (again without any crowdfunding service) for my first CD and did something really interesting for CD number two.

I had landed a regular gig at a local mall playing in the rotunda every Saturday. A few months before Christmas time, I was talking to the mall manager and she asked me if I knew of any cool items the mall could buy that Santa could give away when kids came to visit. In the past, they had given away coloring books and even DVDs. I suggested they give away my Christmas CD (oops, I didn't have a Christmas CD), and they said yes. They ordered 1,000 copies, and I used the money to record and print 2,000 CDs. I gave them 1,000, and I kept 1,000 to sell. This was a super deal because all the kids who got a CD from Santa were exposed to Mr. Billy! My website and contact info was in every CD.

Everything I did was in some way related to getting more gigs and selling more music. For a while, I wrote a "making music with kids" column in a children's and family magazine that let me put my monthly schedule at the end of each story. I framed the schedule with dotted lines so parents could clip it and stick it on the refrigerator with a magnet.

Between my regular TV and media blitzing in the first few years of my career, people still think of me as the guy on TV and newspapers. For me, timing was everything; real rock music for kids was pretty newsworthy in itself—something no one in my area had done before. I didn't have to reinvent the wheel. I just tried to give my projects a 10 percent spin, addition, or makeover to truly make them mine.

I was now booking shows at schools, festivals, fairs, and libraries as a result of finding a creative way to get my CD into the hands of my target market. But it was libraries that changed the way I made and sold music forever.

A Library of Ideas

Every summer, libraries across the nation do something called summer reading programs. Most libraries share a particular theme each year. For instance, they've used "Laugh it up @ your library," which was a comedy theme; "Catch the reading bug @ your library" with insects; and "Dig into books @ your library," which was a theme for things found underground. For a few years, so I could book more library shows, I would create a show for libraries based on the theme. In case you're wondering, summer reading library concerts (in fact, library concerts in general) are *not* limited to kids' music.

Then, one year, I decided to record a CD of songs that went with the national library theme. I contacted libraries all over the country to let them know about the CD and show. I booked a lot of shows, and I sold a ton of CDs. One state library association in Nebraska ordered a CD for every library in the state, about 700 copies as I recall. From that point on, I was hooked. I've made a summer library-themed CD every year since.

The 12 CDs in 12 Months Challenge

By 2011, I had been recording a CD a year for the libraries, and I wanted to do something really *big* to challenge myself. Inspired by an artist named Jonathan Colton, who did a song a week for a year, I told all my fans, friends, followers, and peers that I was going to record and release 12 CDs with 12 songs each in just 12 months in 2012. I figured if he could do that, I could do this. Beginning the second week of January 2012, I began writing, recording, designing, mastering, and releasing CDs. It was a huge undertaking but I had a monthly plan.

- *Week one:* Pick a theme, write, co-write, or find twelve songs that fit the theme.

- *Week two:* Record two songs a day on my Mac or iPad.

- *Week three:* Do artwork on my iPad, mix, master, and upload to Kunaki*.

- *Week four:* Rest: Do normal stuff with the family— no writing or recording.

Kunaki is an on-demand CD replication service. You can order as few as one CD at a time or hundreds, very inexpensively. If it wasn't for this service, I could never have released hard copies. Although they have no customer service, I still recommend them highly.

That was my plan, and it mostly worked, until summer when my big gigging season started. I was playing four to six shows a week June through August and got very behind. I had been blogging the whole experience (*www.12cdsin12months.com*) and communicating with my fans and friends in the business, and once they realized I might not make my goal, people started to offer their help. I ended up having to do the last five CDs in two months.

Professional songwriter Dave Kinnion (from the Jim Henson Company, Disney, Pixar) and his son Oliver started writing songs and collaborating with me. Dave vowed to write three songs a week for my themes until I was done. And he did. Many musicians from around the world that I met on Facebook and Twitter would record parts and send them to me so I could add them to my tracks; it was awesome and really got everyone involved. The final CD of the twelve was a tribute to everyone who was a part of the project, called "A Little Help from My Friends"; it features nothing but collaborations and duets.

When you are trying to record so much music in a short period of time, you get really creative. I recorded songs at sound checks, in hotels, restaurants, cars (parked and moving!)...you name it. I did a lot of preproduction on my iPad (keyboards and drum programming). Then I moved the projects over to an old beat-up MacBook (not Pro) using Garage Band, a guitar interface, and a USB mic. I became great at recording really fast.

All twelve CDs (and the rest of my catalog) were added to the CD Baby store as they were ready. I choose CD Baby for all my online distribution because for a one-time fee they put your music everywhere. Many of the CDs I recorded during this time made it into the CD Baby Top Sellers charts.

Lessons in Marketing

I did this all without the use of traditional advertising. I don't believe in advertising; I believe in marketing. There is a huge difference. If you create great, marketable, "can't live without" songs and albums that have the *right* titles and cover artwork that scream *you need me* to the right audience, sales will follow.

Because I recorded at home and did my own artwork and design, the only money I had to spend was for cover song licenses and hard copies on demand. Speaking of design, a CD cover can help to sell your music or lose a sale. Remember, in today's times, your album must look great the size of a postage stamp. If people don't know who you are, maybe consider titling your album in a way that explains your style or what the songs are about in a larger font than your band name or logo. Do some research and find out what type of images your fan base relates to and use that. Stay away from anything that would turn them off. I learned that (and most everything else important) the hard way.

The biggest lesson I learned that led to my sales (and booking) success was to *stop selling "me."* If you check out my biggest-selling albums, you will see that the titles are about the *theme* of the album. My name is almost not visible, and certainly not at the top of the product. I created albums, songs, and themed shows that were super desirable, no matter who the artist was. I repeat: Once I took *me* out of the spotlight, I became a success.

Eventually, I became the "go-to" guy in my musical field, and people began to look for me. They trusted me and expected me to deliver what they needed musically. The rise of social media helped to identify like-minded music buyers and users. If you can entertain and interest people on Facebook and Twitter, they might just follow, share, and look forward to what you have to say (or sing and play).

Here is the interesting part of the entire experiment. As I went along, my songwriting got better, my production got better, and I learned how to sing well. Another weird thing happened: My sales went through the roof. Most bands sell only 100 or less units of each CD or album, and make pennies on streaming services. There were months I was able to support myself on music sales and streaming income alone. It seemed like the more music I made, the more I sold. Except for my blog, email list, and social media, I did not advertise, promote, or market any of these CDs as much as I had my previous efforts. I did no cold-calling on distributors, venues, or anything like that. But I was building buzz online (with bloggers and podcasters) and offline at shows and local media. The whole twelve CD project got a lot of attention.

Right from the start, at every gig, I signed up people for a mailing list and, later, an email list. By the third year of doing Mr. Billy shows, I had 8,000 people on my list (fans and clients) and sent out regular messages one or twice a month. Though I use less email now, I still use Facebook, Twitter, and direct texts to fans.

In the early days, we didn't offer any "perks" to join my list. The list was the perk! I don't always offer a sign-up bribe online or at a show, but that changes from time to time. The best way to build a list was, and still is, to be in front of your fans and get them signed up while they are hot and ready to rock. Remember, Facebook, Twitter, Instagram...all that will all fail one day. You need a way to contact your fans directly; email and text are the most reliable methods.

To this day, I have my website address, social media icons, and cell phone/text number posted onstage. I also encourage smartphone use at my shows. At the beginning of each show, I ask the audience to take out their phones and turn them *on*! I ask them to take pictures and video and to post on Facebook, Instagram, and to text me photos or make requests. Every time someone texts me, I ask if they want to be on the email list or text list.

The World According to Mr. Billy

I see no end to the Mighty Mr. Billy machine. I love kids, I love to do these shows, I love to make these CDs, but I am always evolving and changing. As I see it, there are two different approaches to making "public" music.

- *Make music for you.* Do what you want and hope you find a following that is willing to buy into what you have to sell.

- *Make music for an existing group.* Do something you dig that you know someone else will dig (and buy) too!

From my experiences, it's easier to find a tribe than to create one. Be flexible and willing to grow. If you gain the trust of your followers, maybe they will grow with you.

Sometimes I refer to myself as "The David Bowie of Kids Music." Music is music to me; it's the lyrics that make it kid or family appropriate. A lot of the music I make now sounds just like the Billy Zack and the Attack stuff; it's just about dinosaurs and fire trucks instead of drinking and crazy women.

For my next great adventure, I am getting ready to expand my reach and record my first nonkids music and do live shows for people over eighteen since my Billy Zack days. My son and I have been writing and recording nerdy geek songs about zombies, Star Trek, sci-fi, fantasy, horror, and comic books, and plan to do shows at comic and sci-fi conventions. Once again, I have a built-in fan base to tap into. People are crazy about this stuff, so I expect we should be successful at this as well. Remember, success is a choice, and I choose to be successful. How about you?

I'll close with five takeaways—things to remember that sum up my approach to a long and successful music career:

- *Singers sing, players play, writers write...always.* Remember to share your talents.

- *Never fear change.* You are changing all the time. Your music, your sound; your fans are changing every second. Go with the flow because change is good; change is natural. If you have enough change, you can get anything you want.

- *There is nothing you have seen another human being do that you cannot do.* You *do not* have to reinvent the wheel. Make it 10 percent new, and run with it.

- *Every time you make a decision, know* why *you want to do it, what you are going to give up to do it, and what you will do when the going gets tough.*

- *You don't have to play, sing, or write the best songs; you need to find the best audience for what you play, sing, and write.* Know your target audience!

Thank you for giving me the chance to tell my story. Maybe I'll be reading about you in the next *How They Sell Music* book. Wouldn't that be cool?

Yours Truly,

mr Billy

William Charles Grisack III
aka The Mighty Mr. Billy, aka Billy Zack

I HANG OUT HERE

www.MisterBilly.com

Facebook: Facebook.com/
MrBillyRocks

Twitter: @MisterBilly

YouTube: YouTube.com/
MisterBillyRocks

CD Baby: www.cdbaby.com/
Artist/MrBilly

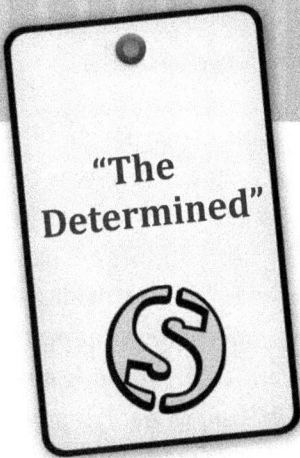

CHAPTER SEVEN

"The Determined"

LISA LAVIE

How to Take Charge of Your Career and Make Your Dreams a Reality

From Montreal, Lisa Lavie is a singer-songwriter who started her career on a cross-country tour that took her right out of high school. She has conquered several unexpected bumps on the path to fame and establishing her loyal following that has led to her current world tour with Yanni and Trans-Siberian Orchestra. Lisa discusses pioneering YouTube for record-label recognition and explains how she took unfortunate-looking circumstances and turned them into a foundation for a lifelong career.

THE INTERNET IS A HUGE PART OF ALL OUR LIVES TODAY, BUT FOR ME, IT HAS BEEN responsible for an incredible portion of my career. It's what got me where I am today. But finding success was *anything* but simple.

I discovered I could sing around the age of 10. I found out in school, or rather one of my teachers, Mr. Terry Clahane, did. There was a school play being organized that had a singing part in it, and my teacher asked kids in the class to audition. Shy and apprehensive about my voice, there was no way I was going to volunteer to sing. I'd never sung a note in my life except for the occasional happy birthday. So I hid behind the boys on the other side of the room, hoping that I wouldn't get called out. No such luck: One of my friends shouted, "Lisa's hiding; she's over there!" And just like that, I had the attention of every person in the room. My teacher said, "Lisa, I'd love for you to sing." And so I did.

"Somewhere Over the Rainbow" was the song. I was so nervous, but I sang anyway, and at the point where I was supposed to stop, my teacher encouraged me to continue singing until the song finished. When it ended, he told me I got the part. I was shocked. I had never sung before, and I just got a part in the school musical. I couldn't believe it!

I guess you could say that was the start of my musical career. I loved Brian McKnight, Mariah Carey, and Boys II Men, and still do. I started singing their songs in my room all the time, never having taken vocal lessons or formal training. I took inspiration from my favorite artists, thinking of them as my teachers. I'd put their music on and sing along and try to change and embellish on their styles, creating my own sound as best I could. I never felt like I needed to be properly trained when I was learning so much from just listening to them; and also maybe because I didn't think my singing was going to go anywhere.

An Early Start

Fast forward a few years to when I was 16. I started fiddling with the piano, coming up with melodies, dabbling and trying my hand at songwriting, not knowing what I was really doing. I just knew that I wanted to sing and maybe record my own demo or an EP and send it out to producers. I didn't have the kind of money to buy studio time and properly record a song, so I saved all I could from what I earned working as a cashier.

But my brother Danny, better known as DJ Devious, had some connections in the music industry. One of his DJ buddies was in this insanely popular French hip-hop group that was blowing up on the charts, called Dubmatique. My brother found out they were looking for a female vocalist to do a cross-country tour with them. He jumped all over that and told his DJ friend that his kid sister can sing. His friend was apprehensive but curious and told my brother that he wanted to hear me before presenting me to his management. I met him, sang a verse of a song, and before I knew it, Dubmatiques' manager Tyrone Foster wanted to meet me.

My brother drove me out to a studio in downtown Montreal where I met Tyrone. I nervously sang the intro of "Hold On" by En Vogue, and as soon as I finished singing, he told me I got the part. Almost too good to be true, still in high school, and here I was about to leave school and go on a cross-country tour.

I never had doubts about leaving high school, though I don't think the same can be said about my mother. My friends were so excited and couldn't believe that I was about to head out on tour, my mother was so sad that I wouldn't be continuing my education...and me? I was amazed. Who studied geography by sitting in a room? I'd learn about the world and more on the road, actually living and experiencing it, not looking at it through the pages of a textbook. Blown away and so thrilled at the prospect, I could barely contain myself.

On tour, I traveled across Canada with a small group of mostly men who were a lot older than me. Different cities, different hotels, fans, singing on stage; it was spectacular. I was surrounded by a kaleidoscope of vastly different experiences. They treated me like their little sister, respected me, looked out for me, and sheltered me. It was great.

A Tough Lesson

But let's back up. I didn't get this cross-country tour right out of the starting gate. Between the ages of 10 and 16, from the point where I discovered my love for singing and being hired as a back-up vocalist, I wasn't actively pursuing music to make a career out of it. I was trying to strengthen my abilities and practice writing my own songs, while trying to hold down my first job and save some money.

I was introduced to a few local songwriters around town through mutual friends. I hit it off with one of them and showed him some of my ideas. He really liked one song in particular and helped me co-write it. It was the first song I ever wrote, and it was called "Guys Are All the Same." Fitting for a 16-year-old girl, isn't it?!

One of his friends who was also a songwriter approached me and told me that he believed in my abilities and liked my work. He wanted us to write and record some songs together. He even told me that a few of his songs that I had heard and liked were mine to record if I wanted them, and they'd go toward my album. I was floored! It was such an incredible feeling to know that people in the music industry believed in me and were willing to and almost insisted on helping me. They came to the studio with me every day while I was recording songs. Being the green little girl that I was, I trusted blindly. I worked so hard and saved all my money—$5,000 from my job as a cashier—to buy studio time and record my tracks. I had a total of five songs sung and recorded by me, two of which I had co-written.

On the last day of recording, I walked into a weird, almost eerie vibe in the studio. The two songwriters were sitting there, brooding and serious. They told me gently and without much premise that the songs I recorded—the ones I had sung and worked so hard on, the ones I was so unbelievably excited for—were going to be taken from me because they had the opportunity to place them with bigger artists. They had contacts with managers of artists like Britney Spears, and they were very much interested in her singing what they had told me were going to be *my* songs.

Those songs ended up being recorded by other artists. One of them was a number-one hit for a very popular artist in Quebec at the time. I found that out as I was walking through the mall one day and heard her version of my supposed song on the radio. The song was sung exactly how I recorded it originally.

Same background vocal ideas, riffs, just a different voice to the beat. All my ideas, my money, my time and energy wasted, and I never got a single penny for it.

That experience taught me that you can't blindly trust anyone. You have to be diligent and cautious at all times. I wish I would have had someone in my corner guiding me, making sure I had a written agreement in place, but I didn't. I was young and inexperienced, and I never thought that I'd be taken advantage of like that.

Having said that, don't ever let yourself believe that if one thing doesn't work out, nothing ever will. Don't lose hope. Right after I'd lost faith in the music industry and been hurt pretty bad, the opportunity to work for Dubmatique came along. Life works in mysterious ways, and you never know what could happen when you least expect it and turn everything around.

A Golden Opportunity?

The tour ended when I was 18. Being a passionate person, there were so many different things I was enthusiastic about—music, I found, was just one of them. There wasn't a predetermined next step for me, but I wasn't depressed or devastated that the tour had ended. I wondered what was next after that exciting roller coaster, but I wasn't beating myself up going crazy thinking, "What in the world am I going to do now?"

Not knowing what was in store for my future, I went with the flow and where life took me. It just happened to be to the karaoke business. I sang at this karaoke bar one night, and the owner approached me to hire me as a karaoke DJ. Wanting to keep as close to music as possible, I agreed.

Working at different bars, clubs, and events was a fun time for me. It seemed like an endless party. But after a year and a half, I decided I'd had enough. I was presented with the opportunity to buy into the company and I accepted. As with everything I do, I invested my all into the company and went full force. We had eleven karaoke DJs working for us, and within no time, Harmony Karaoke was a booming company that spread throughout Montreal.

Working one day at a time, living my life while my karaoke company was thriving, I didn't expect anything with my singing career to come back around. I was so disillusioned from my past experiences with the cheating songwriters that I ended up not sending any of my demos to record labels. But apparently, my demo of those five songs somehow made its way from Montreal to Los Angeles.

A manager named Brandon Reister reached out to me one day, saying he had forwarded my demo to a guy in the industry that he knew, and he was very interested in working with me. Skeptical at first, I did what any person would do, I ignored it. Insistent until I gave in, he went ahead and connected me to this insanely successful songwriter. (I can't divulge his name, so let's call him "Ken.") He had worked with one of my idols, written for her, and produced several of her records. When I saw the call coming in from him, I was in a mall with my cousin Lyne, squealing and jumping all over the place.

He insisted he wanted to hear my voice clear and pure, without any compressors or touch-ups, so I sang a verse of one of the songs I wrote. After singing to him, I had a minor freak-out when he asked me to come to California because he was interested in meeting in person. My cousin overheard everything because she had her ear pressed up against the phone and was losing her mind as much as I was. We hung up the phone, and Lyne and I immediately started planning our trip. There was no way I was going to go out to Cali alone, and who else to take that trip with me than my partner in crime?

Within five minutes, I was calling Ken back to inform him that I'd be coming to California with my cousin the following day. He was thrilled, and we rushed off to pack our clothes and tell our parents. I left the next day, all set to begin a new chapter of my life.

I arrived in Santa Barbara, and soon I was face-to-face with Ken himself. Excited and nervous, I was ready to embark on what I thought was a journey to the ultimate dream. What was going to be a week-long trip to get to know each other better and collaborate on a few songs, turned into me staying there for many years. Of course, I'd come back home to Montreal to visit whenever I got homesick, which was about every three or four months.

The first few weeks were magical. There was a beautiful studio I was working in, I was meeting new people, and it was all very exciting. Weeks turned into months, and I ended up selling my share of the karaoke company because I was under the impression that we'd begin working on music, but before I knew it, it had been a year that I lived there and didn't have a song recorded yet. We'd write together sporadically or when it was convenient for him. I'd spend my days lounging around at the beach or here and there, and it would seem that Ken was working on getting the ball rolling for my music, but he would give me a different story every day about talking to someone about me, but nothing came to fruition. He was also very much into his own band where he was the front man, and I started feeling like the focus was more around him and his project than mine. The excuses and the excessive waste of time continued, repeating itself day after day in a perfect rendition of insanity. When I'd press him hard enough, we'd end up at the studio and partially write a song or work on production of one we had already written.

Slowly, Ken started cooperating and collaborating with me. It was around this time that I started living my life in California. I began dating someone and making real friends. I was big on salsa dancing, and my friends and I went out every weekend. My life was totally invested in the West Coast. This was also when, after two and half years of insisting, I signed, against the advice of my attorney and everyone else I knew, an all-inclusive contract with Ken.

He was the record company, the production company, the co-publisher, my agent, manager—everything. Looking back, I never would have signed that contract or given him the time of day had I known it would turn into a huge nightmare. Long story short, the album that was supposed to take only a couple years at most was finished and finalized close to the end of seven years.

Perhaps the contract was designed to give him full control because of how he suffered in the past—being allegedly cut off from everything, even after working so hard with one of the best-selling artists of all time. It didn't matter to me. Loyal to a fault, I wouldn't have screwed him over, even if he wasn't the one controlling everything.

For years, I worked on my album, writing songs and melodies only to have them rejected or changed by Ken, just because he wanted to make sure his name was on every song. He had so much to prove that he had his attorney draw up a clause in our agreement stating that his name would be credited at the forefront of every song. It didn't matter if he only came up with one sentence, he wouldn't be credited as such, and he made that explicitly clear. Of course, I wasn't having any of that, and I put up a fight, eventually winning that childish battle. This issue was the first of many signs that things were bound to fail.

When there's turmoil in your inner circle, things are bound to crumble. For the first five years, he didn't want me to write songs with anyone but him. No joke. He didn't even want me writing songs by myself. I would play him a song idea, and he would never say "that's really good." He'd find what was wrong or what *he thought* was wrong with it, and he would want to change it. Literally every song. "This one is missing a bridge, this second verse isn't good enough…" And he would want to "help" me fix it so he could have his name attached to it. If I fought too much, insisting the song was perfect the way it was, he would inform me that the song wouldn't be on the album then. I was becoming resentful again; resentful of Ken, resentful that my music wasn't going anywhere, resentful that I was stuck in a situation I didn't see an escape from. And get this: I'd signed a five-album contract, and five years into our agreement I was barely finished with the songwriting for the first album, let alone the recording, mixing, and mastering of it.

The Discovery of YouTube!

Around this time in 2006, I found out about YouTube through one of my little cousins, Kiyana. I thought it was an awesome platform to get my music out there, so naturally, I wanted to try it. I fought tooth and nail with Ken to begin posting my songs on the site. I wanted to connect with people. The sole purpose of making my own music was to share it with the world, and YouTube was the perfect place. In 2007, I posted my first original song on YouTube: "Falling for You." It was a simple video of me sitting at the piano, playing and singing my song. I got my first comment on it, and I was ecstatic! I replied to it, and little did I know the views and comments would keep coming,

147

and I would keep responding—until eventually I had thousands of views on that video and hundreds of comments. It was crazy!

Next, I posted my most successful and favorite song of my soon-to-be debut album, "Angel." I was replying to thousands of people a day and literally going insane with excitement. The comments and questions were coming in so fast, and in my quest to thank all those who supported me, I ended up getting my account on YouTube suspended because the server thought I was a robot replying and not an actual human being.

It's pretty funny how panicked I was at being blocked from my own channel. I wrote countless e-mails to managers and everyone I could find who worked at YouTube to convince them to resurrect my YouTube channel. After one week of what must have felt like I was stalking their inbox, they got back to me and apologized for their mistake. I told them that in return for all the stress they caused me, they should feature one of my songs on the YouTube homepage. A week, later, in the middle of the night, I received a phone call from my brother Michael. He said with such excitement: "Lisa, get up out of bed; your song 'Angel' is going crazy on the homepage!"

I can't begin to express how excited I was. My homepage feature gave way to a whirlwind of crazy events. My videos went from a few thousand views to a few million within days. The TV show *Entertainment Tonight* called to interview me, newspaper articles were popping up all over the place; everyone was reaching out to me. Ken and I worked to finish my album, adding "Angel" to the mix at the last minute, despite the fact that he didn't care for that song.

For artists wanting to use YouTube as the main platform for their breakthrough, YouTube, and social media in general, are absolutely amazing tools for you to reach out and share your craft with the masses. It's not as easy as it was when I started on YouTube because there are so many people doing the same thing. However, don't let yourself believe that you won't succeed just because you have a bit of competition. Post songs that really showcase your talent. Find your niche. If you are posting cover songs, then I suggest you try and get your videos up as soon as the original artist releases that song. When people are searching for that particular song, if you tag your videos properly, you could come up in the first few pages of their search, which means a lot of visibility for you. Also, collaborate with different artists. Promote them, and they will promote you. You have to be willing to give it your absolute all. It will not come easy. Word of mouth and social media interactions mean everything. Be original, be unique, and be innovative to get your music out on YouTube and all other avenues. If you inspire people, if you connect with them through your music and your talent, they will help get it out there for you. Believe in yourself, and don't give up.

My Breaking Point

One of the major labels, EMI, showed a lot of interest in my project and what seemed like a promising venture between them and Ken's company. Ken quickly shot it down, but not before he spent over $5,000 in negotiating the terms of the agreement between their attorneys. It was at that point that Ken's attorney told me that he realized how unhappy I was but that things were about to change. Everything looked good to go, but then I was asked to sign one more agreement with Ken because something in our previous agreement had expired and Ken no longer had certain rights that he needed to sign with EMI. So, of course, thinking that "Angel" was blowing up and I would be able to sign with a company that was going to catapult my career to the next level, I signed with Ken yet again, only to find out a day later that he didn't think signing with EMI was the right decision. I was in complete shock. How was I bamboozled? Did I not learn from everything I'd been through in the past few years? I was so blindsided that I allowed myself to be fraudulently induced into signing an even heftier agreement with Ken's company, with no way out. I decided then and there that it was over!

That was my breaking point. I flat out told Ken I wanted out. Of course, he wouldn't let me go contractually, even though he knew he was in way over his head. Bound by contract, I knew there was nothing I could do. I became very depressed and felt helpless. I tried not to let the situation consume me, but everyone around me felt my struggle.

After eight long years, the album was finally finished, and Ken just threw it up on iTunes. Just like that, without any build-up, no fanfare, no promotion, absolutely nothing. I had a great fan following from YouTube, and my videos had millions of views, but my album was just up, with no commotion, no way to get it some real attention.

PRO TIP$

BECOME A BETTER SONGWRITER

- *Write with people who are on your level or better than you, and be open to learning from their strengths.* Co-writing forces you to move away from your comfort zone, and in my experience, produces better songs.

- *Learn to think like a songwriter full time.* Inspiration can strike anywhere. Be looking for it, and learn to write simply and tell a great story.

- *Check out your performing rights organization for songwriting resources.* From songwriter retreats to camps and workshops, there are endless opportunities to get plugged in. It's also a great networking opportunity.

I moved from Santa Barbara to Thousand Oaks and continued working on YouTube videos and making the bare minimum from YouTube ads, just enough to sustain myself. During that time, I was approached by major record labels, but once I explained who I worked with and what was going on, people didn't want to deal with that sticky situation so that was the end of the conversation. I was stuck, unable to move forward or do anything I wanted. My hands were tied. I lost the opportunity to work with all these amazing people because Ken was indecisive and afraid. He'd make arrangements with major labels, and when anything would begin to come from it, he would back out.

I learned that when labels and industry decision-makers found out I was in contract with Ken, they didn't want to mess with me anymore. Apparently he had a reputation. It is so important to know the industry reputation of someone before you work with them. Do your due diligence, and definitely have a great entertainment lawyer on your side.

I had no idea what I was going to do anymore, but I realized that while I was still legally bound to Ken, I couldn't let that stop me from living my life.

A New Beginning

Around this time, a devastating hurricane hit Haiti. Like everyone else, I wanted to help those severely affected by the destruction and damage. I invited fifty-seven YouTubers, who I admired, to collaborate with me on a song for charity. It didn't matter to me if these artists had thousands of subscribers or only one. I picked them because I liked them and their work. What I got in return was beyond my imagination. Immediately after going up, the "We Are the World" video was a YouTube sensation. I had interviews with Diane Sawyer, CNN, and other media outlets, and it was spectacular! When the video went viral, the love and support pouring in from all around the world, and tens of hundreds of thousands of views, made me realize that all hope was not lost. Things have a funny way of working out, especially when you least expect them to.

Having cut off all contact with Ken, I was focusing all my energies on YouTube, recording videos and songs and collaborations. It was then that I received an email from someone named Bob Murray. It was a request to fly to Florida to audition for the position of lead vocalist for Yanni's world tour. I'm embarrassed to admit it, but I had no idea who Yanni was at the time. So keeping in line with my skepticism of the industry, given my past experiences, I deleted the email.

Not a full week had passed before I received another email from Mr. Murray. He insisted I contact him and said it was important that I fly out to Florida because Yanni was very interested in having me audition. A quick Google search and I found out that Yanni was an incredible instrumentalist who had over 30 million albums sold worldwide. You can imagine my shock.

I got on the phone with Bob as soon as I could and agreed to meet with Yanni at his studio in Florida. Going in for the audition, all I could think of was how much I wanted this to work. This was exactly what I needed at that point in my life. I went into the audition confident and feeling like "I got this." I left the audition feeling the same way, and within 30 minutes, Bob called and said, "Lisa, welcome aboard, you got the part!"

While the year after the release of my debut album was probably the lowest time of my life, this was a new beginning. I was going to travel with Yanni and the entire team on his world tour as one of his lead vocalists. Nothing could have prepared me for the brilliance of Yanni and his music, and I couldn't be more thankful.

Finally, Freedom

After the tour kicked off and I settled in, I couldn't help thinking that there must be a way out of my situation with Ken. I started doing a lot of research and contacting different attorneys for advice. Come to find out, no one in the state of California can be held under contract for more than seven years and, guess what? Seven years was quickly approaching. Boom! There was my way out.

I waited patiently until the day our contract ran out. On March 5, 2012, I sent that liberating letter Ken's way. It was such a weight off my shoulders. This was a new beginning for my solo career, and I was ready to hit the ground running! As much as I loved being able to sing for Yanni, I didn't want to put a stop to my own career. It was a time of change. I had recently become a single woman. I packed up my things, said goodbye to Cali, and moved back.

I was going to be working on a new album on my own, and I needed fresh songwriters who would collaborate and co-write songs with me. I reached out to a friend of mine, J. Rice, an incredible songwriter and YouTube star in his own right, and also Mike Kalombo, a really great producer who I had worked with a lot in the past. They were both very excited and on board to work on my album. I felt I needed one more writer to round out our group, so I did the only logical thing: I hosted a contest on YouTube. I planned to fly the winner to Miami, all expenses paid, and they would get to stay with us for four days and work on the material for my sophomore album.

The contestants had ten days to post a video, singing at least a verse and chorus of an original song they alone wrote. At the end of the period, I had over 250 submissions, and as hard as it was picking the best one from all the brilliant songwriters out there, Sami Douba stood out above all others, and the rest of the team agreed. I flew everyone out to Miami, and we stayed there getting to know each other and bonding over our mutual love for music and songwriting.

It was like magic coming together, throwing around ideas and collaborating with one another. All of our energies were focused on the same goal, and the end result was beautiful. We wrote three incredible songs together. Another friend of mine, Todrick Hall, happened to be in Miami at that time and joined us for one of our songwriting soirees, and things clicked perfectly. This wasn't just a step in the right direction for me and my music; it was a giant leap. It felt so much better than the way I had been doing things before.

Over several months, all four of us met again a total of three times in Miami. The whole purpose of these sessions was to connect with people I trusted, letting our mutual creativities show and putting forth our best efforts to come up with something that would blow everyone's minds. These get-togethers were collaborations and mini therapy sessions rolled into one. We would pull up a bunch of different beats and play them one after the other until something grabbed my attention, and I'd say, "This is the beat we should focus on!" My co-writers asked me how I felt listening to the beat, what emotion it evoked, what I wanted to talk about, etc. I'd get into detail about a particular subject, and as I'd tell them a story, they would write down their thoughts, and we'd go to work on the song. It was seriously the best collaboration I've ever been a part of, and I'm so glad I had my friend Whit Padgett filming the entire process as it unfolded.

What I loved about this process is that I decided who I wanted to work with; I wasn't forced to work with anyone. I decided which songs I wanted to continue working on and which songs I'd put on my album. I had control for once, and it was so rewarding. We finished writing the entire album during these sessions, and I couldn't be happier with the outcome! This new album is my heart and soul; it's my personal diary, my everything!

Never Blindly Trust Anyone

For all those times I was cheated and held back, and the opportunities I lost in the industry, I'm still apprehensive about working with anyone in a long-standing contract. The unpleasantness of the days gone by linger still and perhaps is the reason why I haven't opted to sign with a record label to date. I'd put myself in a situation where I don't have full control over my music. I am doing things my way and at my pace. At the end of the day, I have no one to blame but myself if things don't work out as planned, and that's something I'm comfortable with.

Your mistakes are your lessons. I've learned from my mistakes of blindly trusting people, and most important, I've learned that no one cares more about your own music than you.

To all my amazing fans and aspiring singer-songwriters out there, waiting on the sidelines for your turn to walk the stage and make your mark on the world; all those who are exceptionally talented and want to share that talent yet don't know how, I hope this opens your eyes to some of the realities out there.

Never trust anyone with a blind eye. Keep your eyes and ears open. Don't invest your hard-earned money into something you are not 100 percent sure about. I did that when I invested $5,000 out of my own pocket in recording songs I never even got to use. Be cautious.

From my long-winding journey that has brought me to the point where I am today as a professional singer and performer, I have learned so very much. I have evolved as a person and as a singer. I have seen equal parts success and failure. I have seen relationships built and crumble. I may not have thought so at the moment, but every experience and individual I came in contact with molded me to be who I am, right here, right now.

Along the way I may have lost faith in the possibility of having a musical career. I may have lost faith in people and their abilities to be truthful. But I have never lost faith in myself. I soldiered through every curveball life threw at me, and for that, I'm very proud of myself and all I've accomplished. If you learn anything from my story and my life, please learn this: When you take the first step of any journey, no matter what you do, see it through to the end and *always trust your gut instinct*, even if you don't want to!

'Til next time,

I HANG OUT HERE

www.TeamLavie.com

Facebook: Facebook.com/ LisaLavie

Twitter: @LisaLavie

YouTube: YouTube.com/ LisaLavie

Instagram: @LisaLavie

CHAPTER EIGHT

"The Lover"

THE CAB

Love What You Do—
Everything Else Is Secondary

From a humble start in Las Vegas as a music-obsessed high school kid, Alexander DeLeon, lead singer for The Cab, tells how the band went from playing small coffee shops to some of the largest arenas in the world. Offering modern-day, tangible advice, Alex discusses the pros and cons of major labels, timing, and the mind-set needed to navigate today's industry.

* Written by *How They Sell Music* and adapted from our "video chapter" with Alex. As seen on *howtheysellmusic.com*

THE CAB, A POP-ROCK BAND SIGNED TO UNIVERSAL REPUBLIC, HAS HAD NO SHORTAGE of loyal fans since it's inception. They were just a few high school kids, who were in love with music and passionate about connecting with people. But how do you take that passion for music and turn it into a career? One that allows you to travel, see the world, and move people with the art you've created?

The story of The Cab is about a band that has undergone several transformations, career transitions, and still managed to maintain and create momentum. And front man Alexander DeLeon is a beautiful example of what kind of mind-set it takes to succeed with your passion.

It's a journey that begins with Alex standing front and center at a small concert and culminates in headlining tours and selling hundreds and thousands of albums—from being a fan to having fans. It's a voyage about realizing their own strengths, never quitting or giving up, staying true to childhood dreams and accepting the support of your loved ones to create something truly magical.

"I didn't grow up wanting to be a rock star or the lead singer of a band," Alex says. "But Dad is a singer, and my grandma's a singer as well, so while I guess I had somewhat of a natural musical ability, I didn't start out considering it as a professional career."

Alex got good grades in school and wasn't much of a party-goer. He studied, played his guitar, and started learning about songwriting. A few guys at school got together and would just jam and write music together, eventually deciding to form a band called The Cab.

School of Rock

They began as most new bands do, playing at small coffee shops and a few random events, with mainly family and friends as audience. They were high school kids, they had a lot of friends, and they used that to their advantage. They discovered how important it was to build local support and how to represent their community in such a way that they would eventually become ambassadors for the band.

The band's audience grew by word of mouth. The boys would reach out to everyone their age and invite the whole school and surrounding schools to their shows. They never really expected much from it all; they were just a bunch of music-loving kids having fun. Sure, there would be a good handful of people there and they would make a few hundred bucks, but Alex would just turn around and spend whatever he earned on buying concert tickets. He was first and foremost a music lover and supporter, consciously learning everything he could about songwriting and performing by watching those who were a few steps ahead of him.

"I would seriously go to a minimum of three concerts a week. Las Vegas is the hub of all things entertainment, and I loved living there. Local shows, House of Blues, or huge arena shows, it didn't matter; I would be there, first in line, waiting to see my favorite artists play," he says. "I'd wait to hear the songs that changed my life, the ones that made such an impact on me, from artists I looked up to the most, performing their hearts out. Not only that, but every time, I would wait hours for a chance to meet them after the show ended."

Little did Alex know that his passion for music and presence at a concert, front row-center, would kick-start his professional career. "The whole thing was pretty unexpected. I was a huge fan of the band Fall Out Boy, and I'd read a few of the blogs written by one of the band members, Pete Wentz," he says. "Pete talked a lot about this new and up-and-coming act called Panic! at the Disco and their first headlining show coming up."

Curious, Alex checked out Panic! at the Disco's profile on PureVolume and their MySpace page. He loved their music, learned all the words to their songs, and as always, was in the front row at their first major show in Vegas.

During the last song of their set, lead singer, Brendon, saw Alex singing along. He bent down and let him sing the remainder of the chorus into the mic. Alex didn't realize it, but this was going to be a life-changing moment, both for Alex and for The Cab.

Create a Sense of Scarcity

In the few years that passed before Alex would meet them again, The Cab continued to grow their presence around town. They were not well known outside the area yet, but they had created a web of extremely supportive people around them who were determined to help them be successful.

There are always mixed opinions about the amount of shows you should play within your hometown or your region, but for The Cab, Alex explains, that scarcity was the key to keeping people's interest.

"If you are playing 20 shows a month, thinking, 'The more I play, the more people will see me,' that isn't necessarily going to happen," Alex says. "If you play every week, there is no sense of urgency or commodity associated with you. People probably won't come to see you because they think, 'Oh, we don't have to see them this week; we can just catch them next week.' You don't want to be putting on performance after performance that people will forget 20 minutes after they walk out of the venue. You want to create memories, epic shows, and build momentum and desire for your next event."

When you're just starting out and need to get your name out there, you play as many gigs as you can getting your feet wet, and that's fine. But you can't get stuck there. You want people to look forward to the experience that only you can give them. And you can't be giving it to them multiple times a week for years and years.

Paranoia Pays Off

With that sense of scarcity created and the crowd hungry for more, The Cab decided it was time to record their first demo. As they were getting ready to record the best demo they could with what little money they had, their guitarist's mom offered a relationship she thought may help. In typical music-industry fashion, one of the band members knew someone who knew someone who knew manager Kenneth Crear.

As head of Management Group International, Kenneth was manager to several renowned artists, including Janet Jackson at the time. His mom's friend told Kenneth about the band and asked him if he would come watch the boys perform live at one of their upcoming shows.

He came and watched their show a few weeks later. And he agreed: The Cab had a lot of potential. He wrote the boys a check to help them record a few songs and see what they could make of the finished product. With that, they booked studio time.

Once it was finished a few weeks later, they had just one CD with the masters on it, and the fact that it was their only copy made Alex paranoid beyond belief. "I was so afraid of losing it that instead of leaving it in a safe place at home, I had a friend hold it in her purse when we went to a concert one night," Alex says. "Turns out this was a concert that pretty much changed my life, when we ran into a few guys from Panic! at the Disco."

Alex, in true fan fashion, said hi to the band and was blown away when they actually remembered him. "Spencer was like, 'Oh, I remember you! You were front and center at our first show ever!' It wasn't something that made sense to me back then, but I can tell you now, you never forget your first big show."

While Alex was talking to band members Spencer Smith and Jon Walker, he mentioned he had the demo with him. And he asked if he could give it to them to listen. A ballsy move, as he was pretty sure the CD would end up on "Highway Records." You know, where you hand your record to someone to listen to and they don't care, so they just throw it out the car/van/bus window? But Alex really looked up to these guys, and they seemed genuinely interested. So he took the chance and gave it to them.

The next day, Alex mentally prepared himself that nothing was going to become of The Cab's demo. He was certain that Jon or Spencer would just dump the CD in the trash on their way out, like most bands would, and he would never hear from them again. But a week or so later, Alex got an instant message from Ryan Ross, Panics!'s lead guitarist.

"I thought what anyone in his or her right mind would've thought! That someone was messing with me…this *had* to be a practical joke."

But, it wasn't a prank, and the guys of Panic! at the Disco had listened to their demo. They began messaging back and forth over the next few days, beginning a friendship that eventually led to the boys of Panic! inviting The Cab to their cabin to hang out and play music.

"That night was incredible. We were all just jamming, playing all our favorite songs and our own music. Brendon, their lead singer, would come and join in with me, or he'd take over and sing in my place on my songs, and I would do the same on his," Alex says. "He had actually learned the words to *our* songs; I was blown away."

The night at Panic!'s cabin went so well, and the boys were so impressed with The Cab and the songs they had written, that they decided to introduce them to Panic!'s manager, Jonathan Daniel of Crush Management. And that's where things really got interesting.

"Their team really liked us and wanted to give us a shot. So Panic!, along with Pete Wentz from Fall Out Boy, signed us to Decaydance Records, an imprint of Fueled by Ramen," says Alex. And just like that the organic relationship they had built with Panic! had led The Cab to landing their first record deal.

"We were thinking, 'Oh man, we've made it! We're on a roster with all our favorite bands; this is going to be a smooth ride to the top!' Ha, little did we know then, the work had just begun," says Alex.

In the midst of all this, Alex graduated high school, and The Cab began work on their debut album. "Whisper War" was the product of insane amounts of hard work, amazing collaborations with Brendon, Pete, and Patrick, and a whole lot of love and fast learning over several months.

Quality Over Quantity

"A great song is the beginning," says Alex. "The music is the foundation and the platform and everything else stems from that." Understanding the importance of quality over quantity when it comes to writing their music is something that has always set The Cab apart. They know that no legitimate deal is given because the artist has written 200 OK-sounding songs, but doesn't have at least two to five *great* songs. So Alex takes his time and careful consideration with every song he creates, making sure it's the quality his fans expect and deserve.

In looking for a publishing or label deal, The Cab knew that people don't have time to listen to an entire catalog. In two to three songs, he was able to show an accurate representation of what The Cab is as a brand and what kind of music they create. It is better to leave people hanging, wanting more from you, than giving them too much filler content that doesn't impress.

"People want to listen to the best artist and the best songs on the market, and if you can't provide that, with the number of options available, they'll just latch onto someone who has them," Alex says. "You've got to work each day like someone is trying to take it from you."

Timing Is Everything

With Decaydance, The Cab did arena tours with some of the best and biggest names in the industry. It was an amazing run, but months down the line, it was evident the timing wasn't right. Though the label saw incredible talent in The Cab, often talent and knowing the right people will only take you so far. The timing is crucial and the ultimate dictator. No matter how many things you may have working in your favor, you have to realize that sometimes timing is just out of your control.

The band had signed with Fueled by Ramen when the label was exploding with success. They had some of the top acts in the industry, all at the peak of their careers: Panic!, Jimmy Eat World, Fall Out Boy, Paramore, Gym Class Heroes, Yellowcard. This meant there were hit singles all being released at once and so many tours happening at the same time. That made things a little difficult for The Cab coming in, trying to get the label's full attention during all the hustle and bustle. Decaydance couldn't lose focus on the artists on their roster. It's a 24/7 battle to get them to the top of the charts and a 24/7 battle to keep them there. There's only so much time in a day for a label to push that many artists, and focus on trying to break in a new act when there is that much going on.

As great a label as FBR is, and as much love as they had for The Cab, the boys decided that to get to the next level they would need to leave the label they loved and had given them their first chance.

The split with FBR was amicable. "It was great being there, and John Janick, who ran FBR when we were there, is a great guy who really cared about his artists, but it just wasn't working at the time. And that's OK," says Alex.

Many people have the general perspective that once you've been signed to a label, you've pretty much made it. And that's the farthest thing from the truth. Signing to a label involves the same fight to stay relevant and push your music, only with tens of thousands of dollars on the line. "You have to understand that there will be times when you can literally do everything 100 percent right," Alex says. "You can know all the right people, do all the right things, release a great song or an album, and it *still* won't work out." But there are always options to figure out a new direction, find your niche, and a way that *is* working, and change the plan.

The biggest gift you can give yourself is insanely thick skin. Do not let the "no" define you and your potential, as you will hear "no" ten times more than you will hear a "yes." If artists gave up the first time they got kicked down, dropped by a label, or anything else that can shake your plan, there would be no successful artists. Persistence and the willingness to do the work yourself, finding a way and a path that works for *you,* is the biggest asset you can have.

You pick a direction and your goals, and you run with it until 1) you realize the strategy should change, or 2) the hustle has led you to something better. That will show those who are watching that you know what you are doing, or at least are getting *somewhere*, instead of floating and waiting for it to all make sense.

Know What You Want—and Work Hard at It

When the time came for Decaydance and The Cab to go their separate ways, it was fortunate that the band had been so hands-on in their careers, knowing exactly who they were as a brand, or they may not have known how to sustain being on their own. It's foundationally crucial to know the business you are in and not expect others to know it for you or do the work. It will do nothing but cripple you in the long run. If you are serious about being an artist, and not just being famous, you've got to study the industry, figure out who you want to be inside of it, who can help you get there, and put the work in.

It's far from unheard of, going independent and being insanely successful. Just look at several of the acts in this book! It's a lot more work than when you're not associated with a label and with staff behind you; you have to search for or create the opportunities yourself, but it's entirely doable. So many have done it, and with their second album, "Symphony Soldier," The Cab did it too.

But it was far from easy.

"When we separated from Decaydance, if our fans, the diehards that are like our family, hadn't stuck with us and encouraged us to keep going, we probably wouldn't be a band today," Alex explains. "They encouraged us when things got tough and we didn't know what to do. They never abandoned us because they know we would never abandon them. They've been there for us through everything: the good, the bad, label or no label because we put them at the core of why we do what we do. We have no career without them."

After the split, Alex and the band did everything they could to get "Symphony Soldier" out to their fans. They did everything themselves and they kept touring, focusing on their fans, and including them in every part of their journey. After spending two years of keeping the band afloat on their own and Alex writing the best material he could to bring the focus back to the music, they finally met the right team at the right time. "That's when we found John Feldmann. Massive producer and singer-songwriter, John's a musical genius, and we were huge fans of his work," Alex says. "Our manager decided to send our stuff to him to see if he was interested in working with us."

Although John listened to their music and was a fan of what they did, he didn't have time to take them on, given that he had to focus on bigger projects. Not to mention the band didn't have much money either at the time. But a few weeks later, Alex received a phone call from his manager explaining that John had a three-week window that opened, and if they wanted it, they would need to start recording *the next day*.

It was far from convenient, but life, and certainly the industry, bends for no one's schedule. You get small windows of opportunity that can make or break you. "It's entirely up to you to seize the moment and jump through that window, however small, because it can and it will shut so much faster than it opened," Alex says. "You have to make sacrifices and prioritize because no one is going to do that for you. *You* are in charge of what will come out of an opportunity."

The Cab took that window of opportunity and jumped through it with everything they had on the line.

PRO TIPS

GAIN MORE FANS

- *If you want to be an artist, you have to play shows.* At every show you play, no matter how small, make it your goal to meet everyone who took their time and spent their money to see you. Take genuine interest in them. You are so fortunate to have these people around you.

- *It is just as big of an honor to meet my fans as they think it is to meet me.* Thank them for keeping a roof over your head and for listening to your music. Never underestimate the power of paying attention to someone and thanking them.

- *If you want to sell 1,000 CDs, you need to shake 1,000 hands.* There are no shortcuts. Build your relationships, let people know you care about them, and don't worry about the sales. If you care about your relationships, the sales will come.

For three weeks straight, Alex lived and breathed that album. "I didn't sleep; I caught three or four hours of nap time every night on a couch at the studio," Alex says. "I didn't leave, and I sang and recorded and poured everything I had into that album because I knew our future depended on it." But the work didn't end when the recording did.

"I know and understand how difficult it is for artists trying to make a name for themselves today. I understand how it weighs on your mind that you're not signed to a label or you don't have any backing," Alex continues. "For all those, I've got this to say: *Don't worry about what you don't have and seriously focus on what you do have.* Mentally envision yourself getting to where you want to be. You may never get to exactly where that place is…but with that sort of focus, 365 days from *right now*, your life will look completely different than it does right now, and you will be closer."

You will always get farther having explicit goals than just taking each day as it comes and trying to make *something* happen. When you set very clear goals for yourself, if you do meet someone who sees potential and wants to help you, you know exactly what to ask for. You know exactly what you want and what you need right now. How can anyone help you if you don't know where you want to be? There is a difference between having the goal of "I want to be famous and be on the radio," and "I want to sell 30,000 records this year, play 105 shows, and gain 10,000 Twitter followers." You can't really make a plan for the first, but you can for the second.

As hard as it is for some artists to understand, you can't expect *anything* you don't work for. You can't assume something will just happen or develop on its own; you have to work as if nothing will be handed to you. And if something is, it's a bonus.

"You can't survive with this prehistoric thinking," Alex says. "This thought that you have to live and die by the label; that's just not the case anymore." The Internet alone has given people with talent the perfect platform to do whatever they want, however they want—*if* you can find a way to stand out from all the clutter with a persistent and strategic plan over the course of several months. That's what it takes to get people to notice. Your own creativity is what will attract people's attention, not a pre-written formula. "The formula is dead. With the Internet, your geographic location is also no longer a factor," says Alex. "So what if you're not in LA or Nashville—that's not an excuse anymore."

One way to expedite the level of attention you want is to have a story and generate buzz about it. Look at the artists who hit it big with shows like *The Voice* or *American Idol*. They all have some kind of a *story that makes them relatable*. Look at who you are and aspects of your life that people can relate to.

There isn't a guaranteed straight path that will lead you to dreams and not just one single solution that will work for every artist. We wish there was, but unfortunately, there isn't. So you can't cancel anything out at first. Try your hand at anything and everything, and eventually you will stumble upon something that works for you and your brand. Then, *stick with it.*

Breaking the Top 40

When The Cab finished recording "Symphony Soldier," they didn't have a record label to promote them or help get the record out there, so they reached out and hired independent radio promoter Steve Zap of Z-Entertainment. "Steve Zap was an angel for our band at the time. Not only is he a genuinely great guy, he truly cared about our music and was a fan," Alex says. He got The Cab radio play with the budget and the fan base they had, and together they broke Top 40 radio as an unsigned act. This was proof enough for them that they had focused on the right things and built some pretty substantial relationships and the best product they could.

"We went to hire the same people that a label would've hired," Alex says. "We probably paid a whole lot more, but we got the same results. We approached people who really cared, showed them our value, had a great record, and they supported us because they saw it."

Alex credits satellite radio as the move that probably saved their career. "People think satellite radio is secondary to mainstream radio, and I totally disagree," he continues. "The people at Sirius XM Radio were more passionate about music and the artists that they support than anyone I've ever come across, and they can be a huge tool when you are ready to make a big push to radio."

You only get to launch your first big radio push once. You only get to launch that first album once. You want to make it count, and that takes having the ability (read: financial capacity, tour dates, distribution plan around the record) to support the promotion that radio play would give you. When The Cab kept their traction up and stayed on the radio, that's when other labels began calling.

"We were fortunate to have a few offers, but choosing to sign with Universal Republic was a pretty easy decision to make," Alex says. "They were passionate about The Cab's music and friends of ours even before we'd left the first label. You can't just go with the label that's going to pay you the most. Putting monetary benefits aside, I was going to go with someone who would push and promote our music like it was their own, waking up every day and not taking 'no' as an answer for The Cab. That's the spirit Universal brought to the table."

Fame Isn't Built in a Day

The Cab has continued to gain worldwide fame staying true to what they know works: being present with and for your fans in everything you do. You work your way up. And if something doesn't work, you keep going, and you try something else.

Today's generation of talented artists has been jaded seeing these one-hit wonders, and they want to figure out how to become the next instant big thing. But those artists are just that—they are one-hit wonders. If you want your five minutes of fame, find a gimmick. But if you really want a long-term career, it won't be handed to you. It has to be built over time.

The Cab is already finding amazing success with Universal, and it's clear nothing is taken for granted. "I care so much about those who appreciate my art and my talent; the ones who spend their money on my music and merchandise and interact with me on social media. Because there was a time when I was that fan. That kid at the front row of every concert, the kid that waits hours and spends hundreds of dollars on concert tickets; I was that kid."

Every time Alex meets his fans face to face, he keeps those memories at the forefront of his mind. "How I treat someone who connects with me or my music is a direct reflection of my past experiences. It takes less than ten seconds to be nice to someone, to talk to a fan who's waited hour upon hour for you because you have a song they relate to. It takes ten seconds to make a person's day, hour, month, or life, or just as long to completely destroy whatever opinion they had of you. As an artist that's your job. Your job is not to have an ego."

When you are preparing to release a record, forget for the time being sales and making money off your music. That should all be secondary. When you focus on the quality of your music, what you're promoting speaks for itself, and that's when you win. If someone likes what you've created, they *will* share it with others. That's what people do; it's human nature.

And that is what you are looking for: connecting with people through your talent so that it makes them *want* to promote and support you regardless of anything else. Remember why you're doing this—because you *love* music. When people can see the genuineness of what you do, they'll fall in love with it too. And that sort of love is contagious.

The 17-year-old Alex who got signed to a record label thought that was it, that he'd made it in the industry. It's been ten years living his passion, and Alex works harder than he ever has before, and understands that he is fortunate enough to have the life most artists dream of.

The secret? *Labels, managers, producers, and promoters are only good at turning something that already exists into something bigger and better.* They aren't going to create anything for you from scratch, including your fan base. Your vibe, your image, your sound can only be enhanced and polished if it's there in the first place.

You have to start the fire.

Let your quality, your passion, and your creativity fan the flame.

See you soon,

Alex DeLeon

I HANG OUT HERE

www.TheCabRock.com

Facebook: Facebook.com/
TheCab

Twitter: @TheCab

YouTube: YouTube.com/
TheCabVEVO

CHAPTER NINE

"The Team"

THICK AS THIEVES

Lasting Success Is Product, Branding, and Timing

Based out of Los Angeles, Thick as Thieves blends rock, hip-hop, and pop music. From New York to Portland, Thick as Thieves has toured extensively and dominates the West Coast college markets. Thick as Thieves has opened for several national favorites, including Imagine Dragons, Nas, Bassnectar, Empire of the Sun, Sean Kingston, Matt and Kim, Young the Giant, Twenty One Pilots, and Wale. In this chapter, they show us the next generation of genre-less, crossover brilliance and how to create a lasting career by targeting a local fan base first and building genuine relationships with fans and industry contacts.

BORN OUT OF THE NEED FOR SOMETHING MORE, THICK AS THIEVES CAME TOGETHER to create something different. Something that stood out. Something that pushed the boundaries of everything we'd known before. You can plan all you want, but you never really know what's going to happen until everyone gets in the room and starts to hash things out. We welcomed the challenge. It's Nick and Sunday, Max, Clint, Brennan, and T'Challa, and we're Thick as Thieves.

Stronger Together than Apart

We've been singing together as a band for a few years now, and it's been a pretty great ride. We have all had our individual runs as artists, but when we met each other, there was an undeniable chemistry and sound that we realized was very unique. It was obvious that we would be stronger and greater together than we would be apart.

Back in 2008, Nick was already a part of a band that performed in Hollywood on a weekly basis, but it was an entirely different group of people at the time. Sunday and Nick met when a mutual friend brought Nick her demo tape. She'd just moved from Tulsa to LA and didn't know anybody, but she knew she wanted to play music. Nick listened to the tape, and it completely blew him away.

Nick and Sunday had been hanging together for a couple years when Sunday decided to move to Waco, go to school at Baylor, and start a band with her brother Max. At the same time, Thick as Thieves began looking for a new lead vocalist. A couple of members wanted to move on to other things, leaving the band in a bit of a bind.

At a goodbye lunch for Sunday, Nick mentioned to her that Thick as Thieves was thinking of shifting from a male to a female vocalist. Sunday knew that should be her.

With the mutual interest, they both felt inspired to work together to reform the idea of the band, but Sunday's life was set up to go in a different direction. She'd already enrolled in Baylor and was ready to head to Waco to finish studying there. Despite it all, she knew deep down what she really wanted was to be doing music. It was her purpose and calling, and it was apparent that she should begin a career with Nick.

Then the pieces just started to fall into place. It all began with Nick. When Sunday joined, she insisted they reach out to her brother Max and have him join the project. Max and Clint were college friends with plans to make music on their own. However, after a fateful meeting at a stranger's house in Dallas, the two knew Thick as Thieves was in their future. Clint then recruited Brennan, a friend he'd interned with when he first came to Los Angeles. T'Challa joined later after the band met him at a music festival in Eugene, Oregon. The band found its final form. We were now adequately prepared to make something different.

Defying Classification

We identify ourselves as a rock/hip-hop band. That's something pretty different and new, and that's probably our biggest selling point. We've opened for artists of all genres. Hip-hop, indie rock, and pop bands have all asked for us. Why? Because we take the music and the emotions we love, and we blend them together to create a live performance that keeps the audience coming back for more. It hasn't always come this naturally, though.

In the beginning, we were sort of thrust into performing before we even defined what our sound was. We had to do these shows the former members of Thick as Thieves had lined up, and we decided it was better to do them unprepared and learn what we could from it rather than overthink things. So we went with our instincts and did what we did best: playing music. Somehow all our different styles gelled and meshed and flowed with each other to give birth to our unique sound of music.

 We didn't actively or intentionally plan the way we'd do music. We never thought Nick would rap, and Sunday and Max would provide vocals. We didn't meticulously map out our musical steps and check off one by one. It happened naturally. If you're happy and comfortable with the unknown, let things take you where they will.

When we would get together and write or rehearse, Clint, Sunday, and Max would show the group something they had come up with. Typically a certain part was left for Nick to fill in with his verses. Or if Nick had a new concept he was toying around with, he'd share it with the others and get their take on it. And that's still pretty much how we write.

None of us has necessarily blazed a trail for us to follow or carved a certain path that we stick to when it comes to writing songs for the band. It's what speaks the most about our collaborative writing style. Whatever we do and whatever we come up with is because it feels right and fits who we are. Each of us brings something unique to the table, and this band has really grown legs from us focusing on promoting this music and artistry.

As musicians, it's a difficult thing to fit your creativity and talent into a certain box with well-defined borders, especially when all your influences bleed together in your sound. And while the determination of what musical genres you fall into is more important to the people who try to sell your music than to you as an artist, it's crucial that you be able to confidently answer when questioned about it. People have never known how to classify us, and it's been an issue. However, the more we play, the more we realize our audience sees it as more of an asset than a hindrance.

If it's a good song, it's a good song. Genres are more of an organizational tool and placement on an irrelevant chart. The lines blur more and more every day. We use that to our advantage to be able to relate to and capture multiple audiences: people who like hip-hop, indie-rock, or pop. It's an amalgamation of sounds that seems to appeal to most anyone's tastes.

It doesn't necessarily have to be an answer that people want to hear, but you should be sure and certain about what you sound like, even when it's unusual. If you can't look someone in the eye and say with complete conviction, regardless of their reaction, what you are and represent, then in your musical journey you are a step behind. Music is like any industry in that you have to be able to give somewhat of an elevator pitch answer when someone (especially someone from the industry) asks what you sound like or what you have going on. If you stumble around looking for the right words, it makes you sound more like a floater trying to figure it out, and you're going to lose the opportunity. Define who you are, where you fit, whom your audience is, and be prepared to tell the person asking with full confidence!

It Bears Repeating

When you're trying to navigate the elusive labyrinth of the music industry, you have to be prepared to hear a countless number of no's. That's everyone's favorite word. You'll hear it all the time, but you have to be stubborn and keep at it until that no changes to a yes. We've had people turn us down at every corner, yet we've powered through to see it pay off. When people recognize your resilience in the face of adversity, they take you more seriously. They watch a little closer. People pay attention to artists who stand up for something and push through tough times. It's part of what inspires fans to like them and look up to them. They see a piece of themselves in the artist and are able to relate to it.

There is so much to be said about perseverance and resilience. As you've read in other chapters, these two qualities go a long way in bringing success to an artist. If you hang in there with the best of them and throw enough stuff at the wall, *something* is going to stick.

Thick as Thieves is from Los Angeles, and, musically speaking, LA is quite possibly the toughest place to make your way. If you're trying to make your mark as a band in this city, you have to grind it out, stand out, and be willing to work extremely hard without giving up. Because this town is all about the "no" and filled with talented people who will give their all and more, you have to find a way to be better than them.

Your Fans Are Everything—Honor Them

Sadly, it isn't all about the hard work, though. It comes down to the product, the branding, and the timing. You have to know your market, how to get their attention, and be good enough to keep it. We know bands, for example, who work their asses off day and night but aren't getting anywhere. It's either because their product is not very good or they're pushing it to the wrong people. You've got to be able to look at what you're working on with an honest ear and see how it's going to sell to your target market.

When we first started playing around town, we knew we were onto something because every time we would finish the show, we'd hear our audience respond positively as they stumbled over the words they could muster to define the various ways they related to what we were doing. We were able to see their reactions as confirmation that we were headed in the right direction.

For many of the shows we played in LA, we assumed it would only be for friends and people that we knew. But every time we finished a set, we'd notice that it wasn't just our friends there listening to us. It would be their friends and friends of their friends, and that's how your network starts to grow. You start small and do something different that attracts your audience. When people are entertained with your performance and enjoy what you do, they'll be compelled to promote and support you.

When you constantly engage with your fans and audiences in a way that reflects your gratitude, it helps to develop a trusting relationship with them. If you can be gracious and expressive in showing just how much the support of your audience means to you, it continues to bring them back. Thick as Thieves has a great fan following in LA because we've always taken time out for our fans; we've never dismissed them or disappeared right after a show.

We stick around after playing at an event and actively communicate with our fans so we can get to know them and what they enjoyed about the show. It's all about being genuinely interested in the people who choose to support us. And that's the crazy thing; it's all a choice!

We've never been of the mind-set that we should stick around to grow and expand our fan base for the sake of profitability. We stick around because we want to be invested in the lives of those who are investing in us. On a basic human level, we care about the people who come to see us play. This transcends anything that happens during the show and allows us to develop real relationships with people that continue to bring us closer to the people that matter most: our audience. Anybody with some fraction of talent can pick up a guitar, get on a stage, and sing. But the audience demands more than that. And when you give them more than that, they want to stick around.

We honestly believe that you need to be able to engage with the people who take time out of their busy days to come and see you perform. They aren't there for you to do a half-assed job and just stand and sing a few songs. They want an experience that resonates; you must work to connect on a deeper level.

As artists, you're fortunate to be doing something like performing and getting paid for it, but that doesn't mean you disrespect or look down on your audience. They are the very people who have brought you to this level. Instead, every time you get up on that stage, you have to honor the people standing in front of you. As a band, we strive to do this every time we step on stage.

When your live show is the crux of potential fans' impression of you, it's not something you can take lightly. Touring is where roughly 90 percent of your revenue will come from, so we spend just as much, if not more, time working on our set as much as we do the actual music. We practice every day we can, at every opportunity we get. We pore over set lists, continuously thinking about transitions, and tweaking every little thing we can to make sure the show goes off without a hitch. It all matters and makes a difference. When we put on a show, we want it to be perfect, to be worth the time and money that our audience chooses to spend on us.

For new and upcoming artists, it is always such a boost to know there are people out there who acknowledge and value you and your talents. You can only get that appreciation and acknowledgement through preparation.

Content vs. Marketing

As important as a fantastic live show is, at the same time, musicians need to pay equal attention to two things that go side by side: musical content and marketing.

We've had people ask us if we thought one was more important than the other, and I don't think it's a question with a single answer. You can't say that having a great music video and a strong focus on music marketing is the only thing worth paying attention to. This is a day and age where people first choose to listen to new music on free platforms, such as YouTube or Spotify, instead of buying it off iTunes. Yet you can't dismiss the importance of having content that's attractive and eye-catching. For example, we went all out for our music video "Dangerous." We thought it was funny and so did our friends. That's why they were willing to share it. Content that's attractive or engaging gives you a much better chance of having a snowball effect, and that's what you're looking for.

PRO TIPS

SECURE A LOCAL FAN BASE BEFORE EXPANDING

- *Know your market.* Based on where you start and where you are hoping to be successful, there are certain characteristics that will define those fans. Get to know them and cater to what will be successful, without jeopardizing your individuality.

- *Show your fans your gratitude.* They are the reason you are able to be successful and continue to get your music heard. Your fans don't have to listen to you, but they do—and you need to show them how thankful you are for them!

- *Give your all.* When you are performing, you are performing for your fans (along with your love for the music) who are taking time out to see, hear, and support you. Give them a show that's worth their time and attention.

That said, novelties and gimmicks will only take you so far. At the end of the day, we're musical artists, and that's what sells your music. Having a fantastically funny video helps with getting it out there and spreading the visibility, but people aren't going to spend their money to buy the tune or the album unless your music has substance and relates to them.

With any product, you need marketing behind it and a strategy to get it into the right hands. There are so many insanely talented people out there with absolutely spectacular musical abilities, but they fail to go anywhere because they don't think it's necessary to market their product to their audience or think of creative ways to get it into their hands. What good are great songs if people don't know they exist?

The two facets of creation and promotion have to go hand in hand. There's something to be said about marketing yourself at the beginning of your career, not in terms of a publicity stunt or attention-grabbing tricks but in terms of being smart about how you brand yourself. For longevity in your musical career, you have to make both these things work side by side.

As an artist you need amazing songs to back up your marketing strategies and vice versa. Paul McCartney isn't Paul McCartney because he spent tons of money on marketing ploys and strategy. He had talent first and a product that was marketable. Thick as Thieves has been lucky enough to have Zach Mann, our manager, with us from the start. We haven't had to split our focus between our craft and marketing it. Though we make all our decisions together, he's our go-to guy who handles everything for us so we can concentrate on our music. He's the one who's shot and edited all our music videos, along with helping with every other aspect of music management and marketing.

Are You Ready for a Manager?

We understand not everybody finds a do-it-all person like Zach, and we couldn't be more thankful for him. However, having someone to help you out who understands your goals and brand makes a huge difference. Someone who is willing to go the extra mile for you is someone worth having around, in marketing strategy or whatever they have to bring to the table.

We've had some of the most popular management companies interested in collaborating and working with us, but they follow up this interest with no action. They put up a front, portray this supporting side of them that makes you want to trust them with your life, but they never follow through.

Sincerity is a scarce commodity. If you haven't signed a deal with an elite management company you can trust, the best thing you can do is find a smart, driven person who will have your back and fight for you in any cause you take up. Dedication and perseverance can go much farther than a lazy Rolodex.

That being said, simply getting a reputable manager won't overcome shortcomings in your musical career. You don't have anything to manage if you're only making YouTube videos, writing new music, and trying to get more social media followers. This is something you should be able to do on your own. Managers make money off your back-end profits, so if this is the stage you're at, there is no money for them yet. You must grow with the evolving music industry before you think about getting a manager.

Most artists want a manager who can open doors for them and expose their talent to the right decision makers. If you were a manager who had a family and a life to sustain and you were looking for new acts to work with, what qualities would that act need to convince you they were worthy of putting your reputation on the line, taking up your valuable time, and having enough profit potential to be able to make a living off them? Do you have those qualities? Have you built that value?

Measure your progress and your goals. Give yourself goals to meet by the end of the week, at the end of the month, in six months, and one year from now. Work toward them diligently and make a plan you can show to someone to make it very clear why you are deserving of their help. You should be able to show them how you plan to accomplish your goals so it paints a picture of how they may be able to help you get there. Quantify your goals as much as you can. For example, pick a number of shows you have to play during the calendar year, or aim for a specific return on investment with your social media marketing campaigns. You're much more likely to get better results that way, rather than just saying, "Hey, I'm in a band, can you help us? Here's a CD."

Making yourself known, getting to a certain standing, and having some sort of recognition in the music business is by far the most complicated part and where most people give up. Putting together a project, promoting it, lining up gigs and events, financing and arranging albums and travels...all of it's tough work. But if music is your soul, it's completely necessary—and worth it. From Zach's point of view as a manager, you have to go out on a limb constantly, see no boundaries, and wake up daily with the mind-set that you will not take no for an answer.

If you're lucky enough to find someone who's willing to do that for you, fantastic. If not, then you have to be willing to ask yourself what more can you do to help yourself and your brand. If you have to learn how to shoot videos, take photographs, or whatever else may be needed, you've got to be willing to do it. Never expect others to do these things for you.

Can You Get 1,000 True Fans?

Something we've focused on lately is tackling the college market. That's our primary demographic, but we didn't set out to target this market. One night we were playing a small show at a piano bar for all our friends and family members and an agent from the college booking market walked up to us after the show and asked if we knew what NACA was. He explained about the National Association of Collegiate Activities and the entire process of how they do conferences to showcase different acts that universities may be interested in bringing to their campuses. If you're given a chance to play, you have 15 minutes in front of a couple thousand college representatives who can help you get booked for different collegiate events. He asked if we were interested and said there is a strong circuit of universities that typically have a good budget to bring people in. We gave him a couple of our music videos to look over; he liked them, and he got us into a showcase.

Your show must always be on point because you never know who's in the audience watching you play. The booking agent who saw us playing in that bar opened a new world for us in the college marketplace. Another friend of ours who used to come watch us play all the time is now working for a reputable record company. Regardless of the size of a show, you never know where people's lives may take them and what impact your first impression will have on them.

Before we formed the band, Sunday and Nick played one of the best shows ever at a café, for eight students sitting around doing their math homework. They had textbooks open and everything, and after an hour, they wanted an encore. Those eight still follow us and are loyal fans.

Tech guru Kevin Kelly talks about the 1,000 True Fans model. The gist of this belief is that any creator, such as an artist, designer, blogger, or performer, only needs 1,000 true fans to make a living. A true fan is defined as someone who will purchase anything you produce. They will drive 150 miles to be at a show. They will buy every t-shirt, every album, every deluxe box set you offer. They have a Google Alert set for your name. They will like every Facebook post and retweet every tweet.

If a true fan spends $100 on you a year, and you have 1,000 of them, you're making $100,000, less your expenses. Nipsey Hussle has been doing this in the hip-hop scene for the last few years with tremendous success. He makes 100 copies of his album and sells them for $1,000 apiece to his "true" fans. How do you convert average fans into true fans? The key is direct contact and exclusivity. What can you offer these fans that makes them think you are the coolest band in the world? How can you take care of them and win the battle of their Spotify playlist? What value can you add for the listener?

Cultivating 1,000 true fans is a very feasible goal to work toward. You may end up with a million-person fan base, but if you nurture the relationships that drive the 1,000 True Fans model, you will ensure a solid foundation and a more lucrative lifestyle in the meantime.

You don't have to write a number-one song or lead the top of the charts for several weeks just to survive. You just need 1,000 true fans. Think about what you can do to get 1,000 die-hard fans, and reverse engineer the process to figure out how to start today.

For us, we know the college market loves music similar to ours. So we target them there and start to build the relationship. College radio and college students have their ears to the ground; they're the ones who are listening and looking for new, creative outlets. If your music and your talent is something that sparks their interest, then the college market can be very lucrative.

Thick as Thieves has gotten countless opportunities because of our involvement in the NACA circuit; we've opened for various acts like Imagine Dragons, Sean Kingston, and Twenty One Pilots, to name a few. Colleges these days put on great events and go to amazing lengths to make their festivals top notch. We've gotten the opportunity to be a part of these events because we resonate with the same demographic.

Opening for bigger and more established acts can be both exhilarating and emotionally taxing. It's an interesting position to be in when you're playing for a crowd that's solely there to get a better spot in the crowd for the band that comes on after you. For smaller acts traveling to these college shows, often the audience is entirely unaware of your music and who you are as an artist. It's essentially like a cold call in the business world. But you have to think of all of these audience members as potential fans/buyers. If you're going to sell them on your music, you first have to sell them on your show.

An artist's energy and enthusiasm is translated through to the crowd and is reflected back to you. It's all a cycle. If it's obvious that you're up there doing what you love and you're having fun doing it, your audience is going to want to share in that vibe too. Excitement is infectious and most easily spreads from the front of the stage.

A Long Career Takes Hard Work, Strategy, and Consistency

That excitement is also applicable to the workplace ethic of your band. The majority of the success we've had as a band has come from hustling all the time. When we put on an industry showcase, for example, we make sure every family member, friend, fan, and random stranger we can find knows when and where we're playing.

Industry showcases (shows you do to try and get signed by an agency, publishing company, or record label) are primarily meant for industry attendance, so we've often found creative ways to market to that somewhat unattainable demographic. We did a showcase in Nashville once where we knew we didn't have any contacts in the area. To supplement industry attendance, we sent out five-dollar Starbucks gift cards to every reputable person we could think of in town, encouraging them to have a coffee on us now and a beer on us at the showcase. It was all about getting a foot in the door and making a connection. You have to constantly put yourself out there and build your network of relationships before you ask for anything. Hard work and due diligence, and the determination to keep all communication channels open, are your biggest assets to get you where you want to be.

There are numerous one-hit-wonders who shoot up as fast as they fizzle out, and that's not who you want to be. If you want to carve a lasting place for yourself in this industry, strive for consistency. When you get momentum behind you, you have to run even harder to keep it, because it may only come once.

The biggest question in every aspiring artist's mind is "how do we get there?" How do we approach people and industry contacts without them slamming their doors in our faces or throwing our demos in the trash? The answer, as vague as it sounds, is to be unique. It can be tiring to hear this over and over, but if you're doing what everyone else is doing, how do you set yourself apart from the crowd? What are you bringing to the table that is better or different than everyone else out there working just as hard, if not harder, than you?

Some artists never have to start at the bottom and luckily fall into fame and stardom, but let's get real, that's a very rare bunch. Most people have to start at the bottom and slowly work their way up. You don't want to be one of those people who stop in the middle and don't go anywhere. You want to be at the top or at least be able to have a long-lasting and evolving career.

We've used quirky tactics to get people to listen to our demos, and it's worked because people don't expect it. Along with the Starbucks gift card, we've done things like send birthday cards to booking agents and various management companies. We try to be thoughtful and show our personalities, and send something that comes across as genuine and eye-catching. We've had very positive feedback from doing this because it catches people off-guard, and that's precisely what you're looking to do. It's about standing out and creating a lasting effect.

The easiest way to stand out is through being strategic and meticulous during your planning stage. In anything you do, you have to be tactical and clever and plan your steps in the way that makes the most impact. You need a call-to-action. If you're going to meet or call someone who has decision-making power in this industry, you should be cognizant of what the opportunity is that exists and how you can get the most out of your time. What we're saying is you need to know how to sell yourself. If you talk to an artist, manager, or label, and you're trying to pitch them on buying into your brand, you have to know creative ways to sell yourself. Prospective managers don't care that you play two to three shows a month. Every band plays a few shows a month. Instead, wow them by saying you got a sync in a TV promo that generated 2 million views and even more impressions, and how that translated into album sales during its run. Be aware, though, that it's also somewhat of a courting process. Nobody is a fan of being on the other end of a hard sell. You have to blow them away with what you have done without being obvious that you want to do business with them.

Maintaining these relationships is of even greater importance. For example, a very powerful promoter in Nashville became a fan of the band through an event we did in LA, so we decided to take advantage of that and do the showcase in Nashville mentioned earlier. (*Tip:* Getting into showcases is much easier if you can partner with a good public relations firm.) We kept her contact and built a good, casual relationship with her. When we set up the showcase, we graciously asked if she would approach her contacts and ask those who would enjoy us to come to the show. We realized it was a huge thing to ask. Putting your reputation on the line is a huge deal, and there won't be many who will do that for you. The manner in which you ask means everything, though. We did all the hard work—the planning and organizing of the event, making fliers, and such—and all we did was request that she pass along the invite. You wait for the right moment, with clearly outlined goals, and then make your move.

The same goes for social media marketing. When you approach your fan base, you have to be prudent and strategize, and have a purpose behind everything you do, whether it's on Twitter, or Facebook, or whatever else. Be mindful of the image you want your fans to have of you, create the content that will make that happen, and build engagement to inspire them to share the posts naturally and introduce you to potential fans.

Getting a Label Deal Isn't Magic

When artists like us, who built themselves from the ground up, get to a certain level of traction, sometimes they'll try to attract labels/management or distribution companies. Having previously released EPs and music videos and such by ourselves, Thick as Thieves garnered the interest of a small independent label called Industrial Amusement, which was interested in giving us a mutually beneficial deal focusing primarily on licensing and distribution. Their team was small but dedicated. We knew we would still have to do a lot of the work, but we would have a group of competent industry contacts backing us up.

We recently released our first full-length album, "Love Me Blind," with this label because they are genuine people who have a love for our music and what we do. Signing with Industrial Amusement allowed Thick as Thieves to have someone to distribute our music on a national and international level, while simultaneously introducing us to the world of licensing. New contacts came through this relationship, and we're continuing to explore them now. It is because of the label's support though that we have more time to focus on the creative aspect of our career without worrying about some of the mundane tasks we used to oversee. We'd finally found our "Zach" in a label.

Management and labels, the right ones, are fantastic assets for an artist. Not only do they facilitate promotion deals, but they also help establish and put in effect media marketing campaigns and tours, basically all the stuff that is essential to making our voices heard by the masses.

Getting a label deal wasn't like magic where "so and so appeared out of thin air gushing about how much they liked us and were dying to help us." As we've been saying, it was due to contacts we've taken the time to nurture and grow. We'd kept in touch with these contacts for several years, not because they were involved in the music industry, but because we genuinely liked and respected them. They watched us work and grow for several years, and eventually there was a way for us to do some business together. If they had watched us sit around and wait for a handout and not accomplish much on our own, the story might have gone very differently.

We are so fortunate to be able to do what we love and share our gifts with the world. And we are fortunate to have amazing people around us who believe that our music should be out there. The story isn't over for us yet. There's still plenty more to come. We're going to continue busting our asses day in and day out.

See you out there, road warriors.

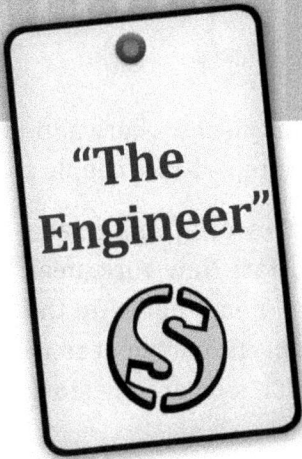

CHAPTER TEN

"The Engineer"

DJ DU

Scratch That: How to Transition from Club DJ to National Tours

> *A 44-year-old DJ carves his way out of the clubs by creating a new path for the way country fans view dance music. DJ DU offers us his insights into how perseverance and art create a beautiful collision. It took him three decades to become big enough to tour as the opening act for names like Florida Georgia Line, Miranda Lambert, and Jason Aldean, but it's only the beginning of a very bright future for this DJ out of Tucson, Arizona.*

SOME PEOPLE MIGHT NOT REMEMBER WHERE THEY GOT THEIR INFLUENCES FROM, but I do. I was born Duhamel Wayne Cassell, in Manhattan, in the heart of New York City. My mother, Edna, is of Puerto Rican descent and raised Catholic, while my father is of European-Jewish descent. In the early 1970s, interracial marriages had their challenges and my parents were put to the test. They lived in Queens where anti-racial comments and threats were the norm for mixed-race couples.

After I was born, my father, Arnold, received a work transfer, and we moved to a town called Niskayuna in upstate New York, near Schenectady. It was a sleepy little town a few hours north up the Hudson River from New York City. We settled in an apartment complex in Niskayuna called Suellen Gardens. That's where my story and musical journey begin.

Confidence from an Unlikely Source

The people in Niskayuna were much more accepting of my parents' marriage. There were constant parties, picnics, town events, and, of course, music. It seemed to be everywhere and in everything. Even the rocking horse in my bedroom made music—the sound of the springs rhythmically squeaked as I played.

Four years after my birth, my brother Yo-El was born, and our family was complete.

When I was 10, my father was transferred again, and we moved into a large rental home near Long Island Sound in Madison, Connecticut. It was a well-to-do town with rich families and old money. But you would have never known that since my parents had almost nothing; instead, we were rich in love.

I moved to my new school, Brown Middle School, in the middle of the school year. It was full of rich, snobby kids, and I had a funny name. It was Duhamel, not John, Mark, Christopher, or something plain like that. I was picked on and bullied daily. I was easy prey because I was new, had no friends to back me up, and was smaller in stature. I quickly went from being a straight-A student to Ds and Fs because of my fear of going to school.

Being a kid and not knowing any better, I took it out on my father and hated him for making my life difficult. He moved us to a city where no one liked me or accepted me. My confidence was shattered, as was our relationship. The hate for my dad lasted well into my late teens.

One year later we moved back to an apartment in Cheshire, Connecticut. It was more of what I was used to, almost like upstate New York again, but on a smaller scale. I made a few friends and seem to be a little more accepted, although I still was getting bullied daily by a kid named Patrick.

One day my parents bought me a drum set. I don't know if that was a smart idea considering we lived in a small apartment, but we had nice neighbors. They put it in my bedroom, and I would bang away. I was hooked! I would put headphones on and listen to all sorts of vinyl records, trying to duplicate the songs. The "Grease" soundtrack, "Jesus Christ Superstar," The Beatles, Up With People, the "Happy Days" soundtrack, "Saturday Night Fever," Styx, REO Speedwagon, and Journey—these records became my closest companions.

In my middle school science class, I had to sit in the front row with my science partner. Every day before the teacher walked in, Patrick came into class and slapped me in the back of the head as hard as possible. It happened like clockwork, and the whole class would laugh at me. I was defenseless and was afraid to report him. I was 12 years old, the new kid on the block, and couldn't afford a school full of enemies. So I would go home daily and cry to my parents, still blaming my dad for everything. Then I would go in my room and bang on the drums to get my frustrations out.

One day, my dad, knowing my confidence was shot, enrolled me in the Connecticut Institute of Kun Tao, a martial arts class at the local YMCA. I loved it! I watched every Kung Fu movie and eventually fought in tournaments just like the Karate Kid. My confidence started to grow. My grades were still low, but I felt stronger inside and out.

Patrick was still making my life miserable until the day I'd had enough. One day I was sitting at my normal seat in front of the class. If Patrick was anything, he was predictable. Like clockwork, he approached me from behind, and I could see the shadow of his large hand gearing up to take his usual swing at me. In that instance, I thought, "No more!" As the shadow of his hand came down, I turned around and grabbed his wrist and arm mid-swing. I threw my hips under him, tossed him over me and over the long science table, and he crashed head first onto the floor. It was a move right out of a Bruce Lee movie! The teacher walked in and saw him passed out on the floor, and even though I was the one who was beaten for two years, I was the one in trouble. I was suspended, but I didn't care—my parents were proud of me for standing up for myself.

The day they let me return back to school, I went from zero to hero. Everyone wanted to be my friend, and the tougher students were afraid of me enough to respect me. I was a small kid, but the halls at the school parted like the Red Sea when I walked down them.

He may not know it, but Patrick changed my life. Without the need to finally stick up for myself, I probably would have never taken some of the risks I took to get where I am now.

A DJ Grows in Jersey

After our family moved to New Jersey, music really started taking off for me when I began helping my brother. He would dance at parties and people would throw money at him; he was that good. Dance was his way of expressing himself, and my parents agreed to send him to dance school.

The basketball courts near my home in Twin Rivers, New Jersey, were our stage; every day after school everyone would lay cardboard down and break dance till our parents made us come home. My parents also built a basement with a dance floor where we would entertain friends and I practiced my craft while my brother practiced dance. My hours of learning how to DJ in front of crowds started in that basement in New Jersey and it's still there till this day.

Along with the break dance culture, there were the big boom boxes, the start of the hip-hop DJ, and movies like *Breakin'*, *Beat Street*, and *Krush Groove*. These movies embraced the up-and-coming hip-hop culture just taking root in America and got me hooked on becoming a DJ.

I convinced my dad to buy me a mixer, two turntables, and some custom speakers. It wasn't the best equipment, but I didn't know any better. It was just the beginning, and I was happy to have what little equipment that I did. When you're first starting out, be gracious to those who help you in any little way and make the most of what you *do* have, even if it's not the latest and greatest. Keep that child-like excitement alive—you get to make music!

Every day I would come home from school and scratch away. I knew I could be the best at this DJ thing. I spent all my allowance on 12-inch records. I recorded mixes and passed them out to my friends to break dance to. Soon everybody was asking me for tapes, so one of my friends suggested that I start selling them at the flea market in New Brunswick, New Jersey. I found a little retail store there, and I sold my music each week at the age of 15.

It wasn't long before I was popular as the go-to DJ in our high school (Hightstown High), and I was asked to join an all-black rap group headed by Anthony (Tony) Hill, a senior at my high school. Tony and another rapper at my school, Eugene Jackson (G-Rock), were incredible writers. One day Tony came to us and said he had set up some studio time at Jam All Productions Studio in Philadelphia. We went to the studio and cut our first single, "I Am Who I Am," and released it with independent label Rockin' Hard Records in Trenton, New Jersey. I was starting to get my feet wet more and more, but there was still no traction.

A Global Education in Music

At this point in high school, I was just thinking about college and continuing to learn as much as I could about being a DJ. The only problem was, it was apparent that no big colleges were going to let me in with my grades, and I was too young to get a job at a nightclub. However, I had an idea: My father always talked about how he loved his time in the Navy, and the military seemed perfect. I could join and let them put me through college. So I interviewed at McGuire Air Force Base in New Jersey and was granted a position as an aircrew member on C-141 cargo jets. Flying around the world at age 18, I'd fly federal prisoners, troops, Special Forces, mail, weapons, nukes, and even the president's limos and communication equipment. Later I flew in Desert Storm, the invasion of Panama, Russian INF treaty missions, and countless other missions I'm not allowed to speak about. My military experience was great not only for my personal development but also for my musical tastes.

While flying all over the world I had a chance to experience music from so many different cultures. I would sometimes go into the noncommissioned officers (NCO) clubs, talk to the DJs, and they'd let me spin some records in Germany and the UK. It was awesome! I learned to play everything, not just the mainstream dance coming out of New York. I was in love with the tribal sounds of Africa and Rio, the throbbing beat coming out of Europe, the wind instruments from the Middle East, and the wailing guitars of America. I was already well versed in the strings, horns, and rhythm from Puerto Rico and Cuba, thanks to my family. The Big Band sounds and standards came from my grandfather which I fell in love with also. My grandfather would come to our house and listen to music from the second he got up in the morning to the second he went to bed. All these sounds set the stage for what was to come.

Facility Manager by Day; DJ by Night

All the conflicts and traveling in the Air Force wore me down. So after my second re-enlistment was finished, I used my GI Bill to enroll at Glassboro State College in Glassboro, New Jersey (now Rowan University). I studied history during the day, but at night I was dying to have a job in a college bar spinning records. I would go hit up the clubs every night and make casual conversation with the DJs. I made a habit of going out into the scene and being a part of what was going on. Eventually, there were some openings when DJs were sick or someone would quit. From the relationships I had built over that year, I was able to work as a DJ and make some extra money.

One of the biggest things that has gotten me to where I am today is being able to put on a show and be truly entertaining. Whether I'm playing for 5 or 5,000, you'll always get the same energy. And I think that is so important. Nobody wants to work with someone who is supposed to be an entertainer and is timid or nervous on stage. You have to be able to command the room and think on your feet when things don't go according to plan. If that's a struggle for you, practice is really the only way to get over it. If it's something you want as a career, whether you're an artist or a DJ, it's your job to entertain and put on a show. I learned a lot about that at some of these smaller clubs and dive bars. It's not the audience's goal to let you show off your artistic talent. Your focus has to be on them.

After college and earning a degree in history, I moved back home to be close to family and my aunt Shelly. My aunt got me an interview with Archer Management Service in New York City. Long story short, I was hired as a facility manager, subcontracted to work at companies such as Merrill Lynch and Charles Schwab. I did so well that in a little more than a month, they offered me a new position either in Orlando, Florida, or Phoenix. That year the Super Bowl was in Phoenix, so I picked Phoenix, and in two weeks, I said goodbye to my friends and family, packed up, and moved out West.

I was managing a huge facility and making OK money, but I would go home and still mess with my turntables. One night I visited a club called Phoenix Live and started a conversation with the DJ playing that night; I told him I loved his stuff. (*Rule No. 1:* You get further with sugar than salt. Never criticize a fellow artist, or anyone for that matter, unless it's constructive and asked for.) As the night went on, I bought the DJ a drink and explained I was new to town and dabbled in music myself. Before I knew it, he asked me to get on the turntables and say a few things into the microphone. All my practicing paid off. I killed it! It was probably the biggest mistake that guy ever made because I was offered the job on the spot at Phoenix Live to replace him. After that night, every day after work I would go and hang out with other DJs, including the legendary Z-Trip. On Mondays and Tuesdays we would hang out at the same spots for industry nights because we worked on the weekends. This was all a result of my initiative to form relationships with other DJs. Had I stayed in the comfort of my home just dabbling on my turntable, I never would be where I am today. It takes getting out of your comfort zone and starting conversations with others. Many great opportunities could come your way, but you'll never get a chance if you stay in your comfort zone at home.

PRO TIPS

NETWORKING TO BENEFIT YOUR CAREER

- *Make an incredible first impression.* There are endless successful and aspiring musical acts on the market. If you are unable to make a solid first impression that will stick with people, you'll have a nearly impossible time standing out among industry insiders and fans. Decide how you want people to describe you to other people, and match that description.

- *The little efforts you make count.* Do something every day to get you closer to your goal, and know what that goal is. You can't be aimless and just want "fame," and expect to get somewhere. Be personable and work daily to increase your network.

- *Even if the results you initially see are not the ones you hoped for, hard work will pay off over giving up or working less than 100 percent of the time.* Luck is hard work meeting the right opportunity and the right time. A continuous production of genuine and well-constructed original content will be noticed by fans and those around you and will not go to waste.

Full-Time Music and a New Sound

I had only been at Phoenix Live for three weeks and was quickly building my reputation when two guys from another club approached me. They asked me to come check out their club, Rockin'

Rodeo, in Tempe, and said they were interested in bringing my talents and energy to it. I visited them, maintained my casual and confident attitude, and walked away with an entertainment manager position at $500 a week. I quit my day jobs the next day. I got to spin Top-40 records in front of 2,000 people three days a week and be in control of a marketing and promotions staff. Even better, I was now doing music full time.

After only three weeks at that club, the same company, GBE Entertainment, said they had a club in Tucson that was about to go under. They asked me to go down and see if I could breathe life into Cactus Moon for thirty days. Little to my knowledge, the market in Tucson was nothing like Tempe. It was a club full of rednecks. They wanted Charlie Daniels, Chris LeDoux, Hank Williams Jr., Garth Brooks, and Mark Chestnutt. I only knew Michael Jackson, Tone Loc, and Young MC. What had I gotten myself into?

On top of that, my life was threatened nightly by huge cowboys who wanted to kill me for not knowing the Hank Williams Jr. song "Family Tradition" or David Allen Coe. I never quit anything, so I started studying country music till I was blue in the face.

After weeks of playing and absorbing country music, I wanted to test the waters. I started to learn guitar and keys, and began to put my own mixes together. This was pre-Pro Tools, or at least Pro Tools was only in big studios, so I tracked things on cassette tapes using a four-channel mixer. This was 1999, and I started to believe that a honky-tonk could be just as exciting as a pop club. I could play what I loved and still play what the crowd was asking for. Why not give them both? (*Rule No. 2:* Never be content or complacent. Figure out what you can offer that is unique, and be damn good at it.)

I took all my influences and started to infuse music together, creating something new and full of energy. I didn't hold back. I mixed Latin, rap, show tunes, freestyle music, house music, and country.

It was all of my life's influences rolled up into new melodies and songs. Within a month, we were the hottest club in Arizona. We had the hottest crowd, money was rolling in for the owners, and I met Kristin, who, years later, would be my wife.

I eventually became DJ, entertainment director, and general manager at that club, and I booked start-up acts like Rascal Flatts, Gary Allan, Brad Paisley, and Eric Church before they hit it big. But when the owner became paranoid because there was a drug dealing issue in the club involving a few employees, and I was asking questions, I was fired from the Cactus Moon. I was devastated. My staff and I built the greatest club Tucson had ever seen, and now I was out of a job. He made some stupid story up to the staff, paid me $10,000 to keep my mouth shut, kept Kristin on as a bartender, and told me never to return. The club closed a year later. (*Rule No. 3:* There is such a thing as karma.)

Down and Out

With me out of a job and Kristin living with me, I fell into a deep depression not knowing how I was going to support us. I had never lost a job. My car loan was late, my home was foreclosing, and I was barely making it. On top of that, my longtime friends at the Cactus Moon wouldn't even call me. I realized, besides my "posse" in New Jersey, most of my friends were fake. As soon as I couldn't give them anything at the club, they abandoned me. Kristin was my only family and friend.

Almost two years went by without steady work. I played country clubs, Latin clubs, weddings, sweet 16s, and small dance clubs for little money. Without me in control, I couldn't recreate the magic at new clubs. I had to listen to some door guy that got promoted to manager about what I should play. (*Rule No. 4:* Always do *you.*) It was getting us barely by, and the stress kept piling up for both of us. I wanted to die in every sense of the word.

I learned something really valuable that had a huge hand in making me the man I am today: Don't take handouts if it will prevent you from getting to your goals and destination. I was so fortunate to have friends trying to help me out, offering me jobs from janitor to flight instructor. But I knew a full-time job would take any momentum I had away from me ever making money in music full time. And as big of a struggle as it was to not take the comfortable or stable move, I knew how crazy this industry was and believed that my talent and work ethic would pay off if I stayed in the mix as much as I could.

The Call of the Lion

As I was about to seriously give up on life, I got a call from a former bartender, Melinda. Her buddy who worked at Red Bull was looking for a DJ who spun country music to do an event in Las Vegas at the MGM Grand after the Academy of Country Music Awards. What luck! I flew up to Vegas and did the event. Little did I know it was a party for Blake Shelton and Miranda Lambert. This. Was. Cool.

While there, I met a manager named Gino Genero. I knew of Gino because I booked acts he managed while I was the entertainment director at the Cactus Moon. I reminded him who I was and what I was trying to do. I asked him if he ever thought about managing a DJ in the country market. He said he wasn't ready to take on a project like me at the time. Still, we had a couple of drinks and exchanged numbers, and I went back to Tucson with the MGM Grand gig on my resume.

A few months later, the MGM came calling again. They really liked my work and wanted me to do events during the Nationals Finals Rodeo (NFR), at the legendary Studio 54, for two weeks. Just like that my relationship was secured at the MGM Grand, and I have been there ever since for the NFR and other country events.

As you can see, most of my "luck" comes from working to be the best at my craft, which is the most important rule of all. Nothing was ever just handed to me as I sat idly by; rather, I put in the time practicing my craft and putting myself out there to form relationships. I took the money I made at the MGM Grand, bought Kristin the wedding ring she wanted, and proposed Christmas Day 2011.

A Life Changed in an Instant

In spring 2012, I received a call from a music festival that wanted to put on a nightly after-party after the main act finished. They heard about me from the local radio station in Tucson (99.5 KiiM FM) and wanted to experiment with my style of music and mixture of rock, pop, and country. You never know where your relationships will take you! When I was booking acts for Cactus Moon, I naturally got to know the radio stations because they would run ads and promote whoever was coming to play in town.

For this festival show, they said I would be opening for a DJ from the Phoenix area, but on my first night I rocked it so hard that when the main act came on stage, they booed him off! The festival management asked me if I would do the whole event nightly by myself, and I accepted. Being a DJ for me was never about just being the quiet guy who plays the music at a club. I treat it like the artistry it is and get people into every moment of it that I can. That has helped me win over a *lot* of positions.

Since I was playing in front of the same people nightly, I spent all day putting different touches on my set because I wanted to make a lasting impression. At the end of the four-day festival, I was asked if I would be interested going to Twin Lakes, Wisconsin, to do another festival.

In my book, that music festival, in the summer of 2012, is listed as my greatest professional moment. It was also when I learned how seriously life can change in an instant.

In the middle of my set at Country Thunder, I was tapped on the shoulder; it was Jason Aldean's tour manager. There were a few thousand people already rockin' to my stage show, but his tour manager asked if Jason could come on stage and do a guest DJ set with me. They had been back on their buses and heard all the yelling, partying, and booming music, and came to see what was going on. I looked at my stage manager, and he gave me the thumbs up. Jason came on stage, and within moments, history was made. Then Storme Warren from GAC came up. Then Two Foot Fred from the Big & Rich posse. Then Wade Bowen, a red dirt artist. Then the event organizer came with cases of beer for us on stage. To top it off, Luke Bryan appeared next to me to join the party, and we all had a "spin off" battle. I can only describe the next few hours as legendary.

The boys had so much fun that word got around within their circles. The next day an agent from The Agency Group, who had heard about my set, flew up to Twin Lakes. He said he wanted to bring me to Nashville to talk about representation. I called Kristin and said our lives were about to change.

Back in Tucson, a few days after Country Thunder, I got a call from Storme Warren. He said he was at lunch in Vegas with Rod Essig from Creative Artists Agency's (CAA) Nashville office; he said that after Twin Lakes, I was on his radar. Later that day, Gino Genero called me (we had still been in touch) and said the time was right to get me to Nashville, so off I went. And holy shit I was excited!

Gino had a plan. I had created a platform (through preparation *and* luck), and now I had something he could take the time to help me build. His plan was that it would be a building process of eighteen months to two years. We first met with The Agency Group who spoke to me in Twin Lakes, then another meeting at CAA. The process was intimidating. Who am I compared to all the big-name acts? (*Rule No 5:* Never doubt yourself.) At CAA, I had met Andy Stanley. Andy had a plan, knew the DJ world, and was young and hungry. He's from the UK and a former soccer player with a competitive spirit about him. After the meetings, I went back to Arizona to talk to Kristin about everything. Ultimately, I decided to go with CAA and Unrest Music (Gino's company) behind me.

Gaining Momentum

One thing I know is just because you're represented well doesn't mean the gigs come flying in. Your agents take a percentage of what they book you for. So if you're only booking for $500 a night because no one knows who you are, and you don't have an album being pushed with money behind you, they are going to make nothing off you compared to the other larger acts on their roster. You still have to do the main work to create your leverage. But they signed me because I was coming up quick, there was some momentum, and they saw potential in the marketplace. (*Rule No. 6:* Trust your manager and agent, but don't be afraid to question.) I worked some gigs for free just to build my resume but primarily buried my head into producing tracks.

With advice from Gino, I started a campaign and created a track a week, which I posted to stream free on SoundCloud. We did this for a year. I would put the tracks up every Tuesday (we called it DU-sday). At first it had no traction, but I would put them out on social media, and make sure they were different. I tried to create a cool story around each one about why I remixed the tracks in that certain way. It was something different than other people were doing. I remember when I would get so excited because fifty people a day would listen to my tracks and then 300 a day. Soon, I was sometimes getting over 6,000 per day just from pushing them consistently, which led to people discovering my creativeness and future potential.

Take your best work, and if it isn't master-grade, I wouldn't recommend letting fans download it (I didn't; you were only able to stream it), but I would create a cool reason to keep people interested and waiting for what I will do next. People have so much going on in their lives that unless you create something that is interesting enough to take them away from that, they have no reason to care. Imagine what it would take for an unknown artist to grab *your* attention, and do that. Start there.

There were weeks I was so far behind, and I had no track ready for Tuesday. My manager would tell me to get my ass off the couch and remind me that Facebook wasn't built during banking hours. It was a great reminder, and that extra bit of discipline made all the difference in the world. (*Rule No. 7:* Never discount the little efforts you make. Consistency in content release is huge.)

Three Decades Later, I Have Arrived

Almost three decades after my love of DJing was born, and almost two years after getting represented by CAA and Unrest Music, I have played all over the world. I have commercial singles out, I just started my own segment on XM/Sirius, "The Highway with Storme Warren," and I've played on the American Country Awards and in countless other gigs. As I write this, I'm out with Jason Aldean and Florida Georgia Line on the biggest country tour of 2014, playing 50,000-plus seat stadiums. But up until six months ago, I was playing gigs for $100 a night and thinking that was great money. I would get to play three to five times a week and make an average of $400 a week, and I was happy. And as you see, it took *years* to get to where I am now. Nobody thought I would ever be playing the stadiums I am today with my music reaching tens of thousands of people every night with some of the biggest names in country music.

So how did I make it in music doing what I love? What gave me the edge—the advantage? Perseverance. It was the times I got bullied. Character was formed those days when I was knocked down and picked myself back up. It was my grandfather's passion for music. My mom blaring salsa music at 8 a.m. every Saturday morning. My dad's love of classic movies like *Singin' in the Rain* and *Damn Yankees*. It was that old house in New Jersey that produced a Tony Award-winning dancer and entertainer in my brother, and an award-winning musician/DJ/producer in myself. Dreams started there, and creativity and discipline eventually took over.

I said earlier that I hated my father for years, but he never hated me. He always supported both my brother and me. I knew he moved us around to make our lives better. I'm thankful we were able to restore our relationship. (*Rule No. 8:* You will learn more from your failures than your successes.)

My best advice is to be passionate and persistent, even when you think you can't go on. People strike gold typically when they push past their biggest hurdle. Be kind to everyone because you may need to call on them one day. Be generous with your time for good causes. Be willing to sacrifice. I lost a lot in my passion for music. I lost my house, my cars, my friends, and I lost Kristin. She didn't sign on for someone who would be traveling all the time; in the situations I got put in, I was not there as much as I wanted to be and did things that hurt. Always stay humble and never let the stress get too far ahead of you. Learn from your mistakes.

Realize not every town has a great music scene. (*Rule No. 9*: Don't be afraid to pick up your things and move away despite your fears of failure.)

But remember, never look back or get upset at things you can't change. You're going to be told no more than yes, and you will fail more than you will succeed. Always embrace your family for support and give back to them. Work hard and then work harder. While you are resting, someone else is out there giving it everything they have. Don't be afraid to stay up all night, work on your craft, and never think you can practice too much. (*Rule No. 10:* Never quit! Even if it takes a couple of decades! Figure out what makes you unique and sets you apart from everyone else doing what you are doing. Even if it remains a hobby, your talent is special, and there are people who appreciate you for what you create. Keep sharing it with the world.)

No two stories are alike, but follow your heart and let the love of the music take you as far as you want to go.

God bless, and I'll see you on the road.

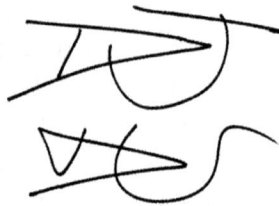

I HANG OUT HERE

www.DJDU.net

Facebook: Facebook.com/ DJDuMusic

Twitter: @DJDuMusic

Instagram: @DJDuMusic

CHAPTER ELEVEN

"The
Innovator"

PETER HOLLENS

A Cappella with a Twist:
How to Build a Career with YouTube

> *Peter is a pop singer-songwriter-producer who hails from Oregon and makes all his music with only his voice. He began his a cappella career halfway through college when he left school to join a touring group, and ultimately landed on NBC's* The Sing-Off. *With his unique niche and innovative use of YouTube, Peter has grown his huge fan base through social media and struck a recent deal with Sony Masterworks.*

IT'S FUNNY HOW SOMETIMES WE ARE UNAWARE OF OUR OWN TALENTS. AND HOW WHAT we are most resistant to can turn into our biggest passion. I have my mother to thank for discovering my love for music when I was 14 years old and failing French class. Mom said that in order to drop the French class—which I hated—I would have to take up choir. Reluctantly, I did. And it was there that I fell deeply in love with music. While I was forced to discover my biggest passion by my mom, it was with the encouragement and guidance of my choir instructor that I found myself as an artist and as a person.

I ended up singing in choir throughout high school, and after graduation, attended the University of Oregon as a voice performance and music education double major. I wanted to expand my musical horizons beyond my studies, so a friend and I started a male a cappella group at the university called On the Rocks. We built On the Rocks into a premier college group, placing second and third out of hundreds of colleges in two international competitions. This was also where I met my wife-to-be: She started the female a cappella group Divisi, which became the group featured in the book *Pitch Perfect*. (My wife's name is actually the first word in the book!)

In my junior year of college, I saw an audition notice for a professional a cappella group in Boston. I flew to Boston, passed the audition, and toured with them for nine months, performing at roughly 200 gigs. I quickly learned that being on the road for days on end was not all it's cracked up to be; it was tedious, hard, and draining. I also realized that singing for a living and doing it someone else's way, rather than making my own path, was not what I wanted. So I quit the group and went back to college to finish my bachelor's degree.

Changing Directions

In my major, I had endless opportunities to observe students record, engineer, and produce other artists. By watching those sessions, I discovered I had a knack for producing music, and I would constantly think of how to do the same thing in better and faster ways.

Consequently, I ended up forgoing plans of graduate school. Instead, I took the money I had saved, bought myself studio equipment, and hit the road in 2002, traveling across the country recording, producing, and mixing for other collegiate a cappella groups I had met in competitions and built relationships with during my stint with On the Rocks. Although it was by no means a glamorous career—recording people in nasty-smelling dorm rooms and makeshift places—I learned that the DIY approach worked: I could record anywhere using anything and make great-sounding recordings.

For three years, I did a variety of jobs to makes ends meet. Some were music-related—like my work with the college a cappella groups and working as an entertainer with my wife on cruise ships—and some were not, like making pasta for a catering company.

In 2005, I decided enough was enough. I made a promise to myself—from that point on, every dollar I made would be as a musician, whether it was from recorded music, singing gigs, recording engineer revenue, or as a producer.

A Turning Point (OR) Turning a Corner

Finally, I had the break I needed that would eventually lead me to be able to make a full-time living off my a cappella music. The producers of the NBC show *The Sing-Off* asked On the Rocks to audition because they were looking for acts to fill their show. We lasted for five or six episodes. While being on the show did very little in terms of boosting the group's online presence, it was the demands of fans who saw me do my solos on the show, combined with my dying father's wish for me to record my own music, which influenced me to start creating music for myself.

After the show, I kept the momentum going by recording a few albums and YouTube videos throughout 2011. The next year, I collaborated on a YouTube video with violinist Lindsey Stirling, which, as of this writing, has over 46 million views. That's when I started being able to do my solo career full time.

Why YouTube?

The reason I chose YouTube as a distribution platform for my music is because I've been a computer and Internet geek all my life, so it seemed a natural for me. I saw the people who are now my friends, like country-pop artist Tyler Ward and violinist Lindsey Stirling, succeed at such a high level on YouTube, so it was a no-brainer for me to follow suit. I've always tried to look at other people succeeding objectively and learn to apply parts of what they're doing to my own career. If you look at the progression of my videos on YouTube, at first they come across as imitations, but now they're different and unique to who I am as an artist and a musician. Each one also has my added twist on it by being "the guy that makes everything you hear with just his mouth."

Survival in the music industry is not just about evolving, but *strategically* evolving to bigger and better things. It's about trial and error and understanding as well as interpreting what gets accepted by the masses and then giving it your own spin.

With my music, I've always tried my best to be dependable. I create music videos for the songs requested by my "Hollens family," and I try to put them up as soon as I can so there isn't a super long break between content releases. The fans are greedy when it comes to good content, and it's always been my goal to try and deliver.

I'm constantly reaching out to my audience, asking if they like this, or is this a song they would like me to sing, or what are the genres they like? If a ton of people ask me to sing a particular song within the span of a week, heck, yes, I'm going to create that. I get to create music for a living, so I'll do whatever song my fans like if it makes them happy.

I was already active on social media websites when I landed on *The Sing-Off*. I started with close to 2,300 people on my Facebook page, and I was equally active on Twitter during the show's airing. I responded to almost everyone, even the negative comments. I replied and tried to change their opinions and interact with them in any manner I could to show them I was a nice guy. So when I posted my first YouTube video, a Rihanna mash-up, which makes me cringe and want to take it down every time I see it, I already had some fans who could get me some good momentum on my view count.

My biggest strength has been engaging my audience and my community. I spend 90 percent of my time talking to my fans and followers on social media. I love that one-on-one interaction, so they can see that I'm not much different from them. I love making people happy. If that means following someone on Twitter or replying to an email from a fan, I will do that as much and as often as I can.

Expand through Collaborations

As an artist, one of my strong suits is the value I bring when I collaborate with another artist. Because I make all my music with only my mouth (the tracks, the beats, harmonies, everything), I offer an unexplored niche to a collaborator.

When I collaborate I bring as much value to the table as possible: I produce the entire video—the arrangement, recording, editing, mixing, mastering (on audio side), hiring and paying for the video team concept, filming, and color correcting. The only thing I ask in return is for my collaboration partner to share our work with their audience in the hope that they find my music appealing and start listening to it.

Many musicians consider other artists their competitors or rivals, but that never made much sense to me. I think of them as my peers, and I want them to succeed as much as I want myself to succeed. You bring each other up in the process. When I have other artists in my studio either making music or making videos together, I do the best I can to help them reach their maximum potential. I honestly believe that the only way to survive in this world is to help build up the entire ecosystem. You create more opportunities for all of us that way. After all, opportunity is what all of us really want!

Working in tandem is especially important for YouTube-centric artists like myself. Everyone who uses the Internet as the basis for their career needs to acquire a fan base to get their music heard, and collaborating with fellow artists is a sure-fire way to do so, or at least expand your audience.

When you ask another artist to collaborate, though, you should have a clear idea of what you're asking for. Going up to someone and just randomly saying, "Hey, I want to collaborate with you," is probably not going to get you the sort of response you were hoping for.

Let the other person know what you will bring to the table and what your idea is. It doesn't just have to be your singing skills. It could be someone you know who does brilliant cinematography, or is a great composer or engineer. Also, make sure it is easy for them to see why it's a good idea. Collaborating with your peers, not just on YouTube but in any capacity, can be extremely valuable for everyone involved.

Take (Almost) Every Opportunity You Can Get

Learning to leap at opportunities has by far been the biggest key to getting me where I am today. When I got the opportunity to sing professionally with the Boston a cappella group, I was in my junior year at college. Taking this opportunity meant leaving school full time to see what could happen, and I decided to try it. I knew that I was being handed a breakthrough chance to make a living doing what I loved, and even though I was pretty convinced my mom would kill me for doing so, I took nine months off from school and jumped on board immediately. The risk paid off, as it opened many more doors.

You never know where opportunity may lead, even small ones. It's better to try and do *something* than to sit back and evaluate for too long and do nothing because you want it to be just right. It probably will *never* be just right. So always try something, if it makes even a little bit of sense. You will be surprised where those open doors may lead!

I honestly think that taking opportunities as they arise and just going for it, regardless of the apprehensions and insecurities you may have, is the only way to truly make a living and it's something I have always strived to do professionally and personally. It's nearly impossible to make it in the music industry without taking chances and learning from them every step of the way. You have to be able to accept, adapt, and learn from all that comes your way. That goes for the good, but especially the bad.

Listen Up

Before I created my first YouTube video, I had never done videography. Final Cut 7 was the pro video-making tool at the time, and it was pretty much my best friend from 2010–2011. The only thing I had going for me was that I was constantly online, engaging with audiences as well as influencers (anyone who had a bigger audience reach than I did and understood the workflow better than I did). The only way to get these influencers attention was to genuinely try to help them and do whatever they needed so I could learn from them. Since I had taken the time to build a relationship beforehand, I felt OK asking them to check out what I created.

If you are a genuine fan of someone's work, and you share it and engage with them for a few weeks or so, then ask them for a favor. That's the best policy. Don't try to cheat the system; put in actual time and energy to build relationships and you will succeed.

Now that I'm in a position where I have people approaching *me* for *my* opinion, I find that unless you have something unique to offer, you're going to be overlooked. I honestly don't have the time to go through every link sent by hopeful artists. People like me work so hard to deliver our best to our audiences that we rarely have the opportunity to just sit and idly listen to songs all day. Whenever I have approached someone, I've always tried to be upfront about my skills and abilities and what I brought to the table, and that's what has worked.

It doesn't matter if you're trying to get a record label to sign you or a YouTube artist to collaborate with you, if you don't have anything different to offer or contribute, chances are you will always go unnoticed.

I try my best to listen to as many songs that are sent to me as I possibly can, and if it's something that totally blows everything else out of the water, then I'll reach out to ask if I can help them, and I have done that on countless occasions. Sometimes I'll just post a message where I'll tell them that I absolutely adore their work and ask if there's anything that I can do to help. Or if I've gotten completely hooked, I'll cold call and spend a couple of hours giving them the whole spiel of how to brand and market themselves. Twitter works the best to reach me; for some reason, I tend to click on things on Twitter. Email sometimes works too.

Be Yourself

When I choose a song to cover, my first priority is my audience. I pay a lot of attention and try as much as I can to fulfill the demands of my fans because at the end of the day, they are the ones who will go online and click on the links to listen to my songs and buy them. My second priority when it comes to song selection is picking one that will be topical or most commonly searched online. More often than not I use the search engine optimization options available with Google and YouTube. Since Google owns YouTube, it's incredibly helpful.

If I examine the analytics on my cover songs, between 30 and 40 percent of the views on my YouTube Channel come from people searching online for a particular song. So it's a no-brainer to pick a song that's already being looked for, as it increases the chances of being chosen. That said, when you're posting cover songs, you have to be able to keep your creative and artistic integrity intact. For example, if I'm covering a Katy Perry or Bastille song, I have to be able to spin it in a way that it's unique to my sound and style, otherwise I'll just be posting another imitation of Katy Perry or Bastille that no one will want to buy when they can have the original. They would only buy it if it is substantially different.

It is so important to be genuine and true to yourself when you design your brand image. That resonates with people, and it attracts them. You'll find there's no shortage of Lady Gaga imitators who use all sorts of theatrics as a part of their identity and that works, but I find that just being myself—the quirky dad who lounges around in pajama pants all day, making music with just my vocals—resonates with a lot of people. It lets them know that this isn't just some snazzy, well-crafted production; I'm a normal human being working hard to support my family. Your audience will gravitate toward you if what you are doing resonates with them.

The not-so-glamorous truth is there are more fickle fans than loyal ones. This is the type of audience that moves on to better things and doesn't wait around for you to churn out new music. YouTube is a platform tailor made for consistent content upload; it's just the way its algorithm is set up. Keeping that in mind, it's safe to say that there is no shortage of the number of options fans have to choose from in terms of music. While you may think that your fans won't find anything better than what you can offer in terms of music, the fact is, more often than not they will think that others are far better and they won't think sticking around waiting for new music is worth it.

I do covers to grab a new audience, but I do so in hope that someone who's never found something like what I'm doing will look deeper into my music. Then they'll see my original material, which might be something they never would have imagined they would like, but they end up loving it. In the past few years, this strategy has been paying off. I've found people who bumped into my work because of a Top 40 song of maybe Taylor Swift or One Direction, but in the end I've helped introduce them to music genres they never would've given a chance to before.

There are so many beautiful melodies out there that deserve to be heard but are not brought into the limelight because most people are almost force-fed the same old pop/rock Top 40 combination. It's the most rewarding feeling to facilitate music and give someone the opportunity to venture down an unexplored musical path.

PRO TIPS

STAND OUT ON YOUTUBE

- *Collaborate with other artists.* Not only will you gain more views and fans, but you will be able to note what works and what doesn't from those that are doing exactly what you do. Plus, making more connections will be to your benefit in the long run.

- *Be strategic.* With every video you make, make sure there is logic and thought behind it. Making a plan as to the content and timeline of your videos and channel will help ensure greater success. Producing videos should be fun, but you should also be smart about how to release them.

- *Keep the fans in mind.* Remember who you are working for—your fans! Keep in mind what you think they will enjoy and want to see. Your fans need to be your priority.

Is Touring Necessary to Build a Fan Base?

Another important aspect of being a musician, and branding and marketing yourself as one, is touring. I know there are many brilliantly talented people who are shy and uncomfortable with live performance, and I know that most artists preach touring as the very foundation of having a music career. But I've also watched careers blossom on the Internet, with the benefit being that the artist is able to tour anywhere and already has fans. They get to bypass the hardship of living their life on the road for years to build that fan base.

I am constantly looking at the concert and touring aspect of my artistry and trying to figure out a better way to make that work because I believe every artist should constantly get outside their comfort zone and scale their business. Because I don't use any musical instrument and I layer the various vocals purely created by my mouth, touring is a little tricky. But I am determined to scale touring into my business and continue building my career to new heights, always giving my fans something to look forward to.

While touring may be cited as the most authentic way of building a fan following, by using the Internet, artists can reach the same zenith of success sitting on a couch in their living room. The beauty of living in such a technologically advanced age is there are so many start-up companies that give incredible value to the artists and allow them to not only do what they love but to do so with a freedom that wasn't available to musicians a decade ago. It can be YouTube or even a site like **Patreon** with the direct fan-artist relationship.

More and more companies are making it easier for musicians to get their work heard by the masses. On my website, I've made it a point to mention all the companies I feel are most beneficial to fellow artists, along with any relevant information about how I branded and marketed my own name for success. This is my effort to help my peers find the success that I have experienced because I truly believe that there is no other way to make this world a better place than to nurture those who are creative and inspire others to go after their dreams.

Think Before You Sign

I recently signed a record deal with Sony Music Masterworks. Signing with a label wasn't a "be all, end all" kind of thing for me, and I'm so glad for that. Most artists tend to have this mentality that having a record deal is the ultimate sign of having made it in the industry, and that's what they focus on. What artists need to understand is that when it comes to bringing a label into the equation, the only way it's going to be as fantastic as you want it to be is if it *works for you*. The labels want to grab hold of an already established base and then add more value to it instead of wasting their energies on creating it from the ground up. But the two-sided coin is that many labels are still stuck in outdated systems of promoting artists and don't readily change their "programming" from what has worked in the past because there are millions of dollars at stake and no formula anymore. So when they try their best with what they think may work to promote you, and it doesn't work, it's easier to shelve you. This is why many artists create their own labels, retain control, and aim for a promotion/distribution deal instead.

In my opinion, no artist should ever settle for a label deal unless it is based on their own terms and conditions. Even after you secure a record deal, creating a wealth of fans is still going to be *your* job, with the repercussions on *your* shoulders if you don't produce. What you should look for from a label is the ability to play the bank and bring the relationships and international exposure you are unable to cultivate on your own. But if you have the ability to "play bank" on your own, you may not need a label. This DIY route is becoming the "new age" model.

I was able to carve a fantastic deal with Sony Masterworks because it was the next logical step in my career. I had the sales and proof of a successful promotional model prior to their interest. Having previously declined multiple offers, the only reason I went with Sony was because unlike other labels which hold all the power to make important decisions about your music, Sony gives me *complete creative control* over my work as well as the team I choose to work with. With this deal, I'm hoping to cultivate stronger longevity and use their promotion and distribution channels.

It was not easy to build my leverage to the point I could strike a deal like that. It never is! But YouTube was my strength, I had a unique selling point because I make all my music with only my mouth, and I stayed in my corner and pushed and pushed and pushed. I didn't over-diversify and try to tour like crazy, be a great YouTuber, start a clothing line, and try a million different strategies. I picked an avenue, built a streamlined strategy for it, stuck to it, and evolved naturally.

If I had taken one of the earlier record deals, my career would probably have been dead in the water, signing it all over to someone else to run. It's hard to hold out when you get that first bit of interest; I won't lie. It comes down to knowing *exactly* what you want and working toward that goal with everything you have.

Tools of the Trade

Because the music videos I create involve complex layering of vocals, which are all recorded separately, I'm often asked about the tools of the trade that I prefer for production purposes. My first camera was a basic, secondhand Canon t3i, which I used to shoot my first video. Later the video was edited on a friend's version of Final Cut video-making software. I used a cheap condenser mic that I bought on eBay for around $100.

You don't need to spend thousands of dollars on top-notch production equipment to make music. iMovie or Garage Band will work absolutely fine. All you have to do is just begin and start learning; start piecing it together. If you want to succeed as an artist, you have to learn how to do these things on your own. Either that, or you'll fall behind or spend a ton of money.

Being a one-trick pony doesn't fly anymore; you have to be able to do most things for yourself until you have a team to help you. Singers today with a true degree of success are entrepreneurs, marketers, promoters, distributors, and sometimes even their own managers.

You need to know how to record yourself as well as how to edit a video and add or layer audio, or work closely with someone who does, specifically if you are aiming for YouTube. Knowing the basics will never be a downfall. Even if you're just a vocalist, knowing the basics allows you to communicate and speak your producer's and engineer's language. That's crucial! You have to be able to execute your vision yourself so that you can guide others when the time calls for it.

I know it's unnerving to venture into something that seems so foreign, but get on the Internet and look for some tools to help you get started in whichever direction you choose to tackle. For example, my friend Graham Cochrane owns and runs the company The Recording Revolution, which is a free teaching tool for musicians wanting to learn how to edit, mix, master, and record themselves. He consistently posts tutorials to teach artists to produce their own music videos like the pros.

Another tool you can check out is Tubular Labs. Tubular is perfect for artists focused on building YouTube traction and knowing the analytics behind getting your numbers up. Not only does this website provide detailed analysis of all the data collected by your channel, but it also suggests which artist collaborations would be most profitable for you as a brand. It lets you see how well your marketing campaigns are doing, the consistency of an artist's subscriber base, videos views, and a whole bunch of other important stuff. If you're looking to present to a sponsor, this is *the* tool you need to show your impressive numbers. And if you don't have impressive numbers, it can help you get there by seeing why what you're doing is working or not working.

Fans Call the Shots

Moving forward in this decade, I don't think music is going to last being dictated by labels as much as it is consumers who have all the options in the world. The control is in the hands of the fans; the size of the fan base is what is leading to new artists getting their deals. More and more it will be about self-sustainable brands that can create a network of people who genuinely care about the music and the artist.

Wrapping this up, the only thing I'd like to say to my Hollens' family and the artists who truly want to walk this path to make a living, is try not to become trapped within self-induced boundaries. Don't limit yourself to any singular thing or avenue. Learn anything and everything you can about your craft and then some. I hope that the wealth of knowledge that is brought to you by this book and all the artists combined as well as my humble two cents are helpful to you.

Please connect with me online if you have any other questions! I love helping my peers.

I HANG OUT HERE

www.PeterHollens.com

Facebook: Facebook.com/PeterHollensMusic

Twitter: @PeterHollens

YouTube: YouTube.com/PeterHollens

Instagram: @PeterHollens

Patreon: www.Patreon.com/PeterHollens

Snapchat: @PeterHollens

Tumblr: PeterHollens.tumblr.com/

My own FAQs to help my peers:
PeterHollens.com/faqs/

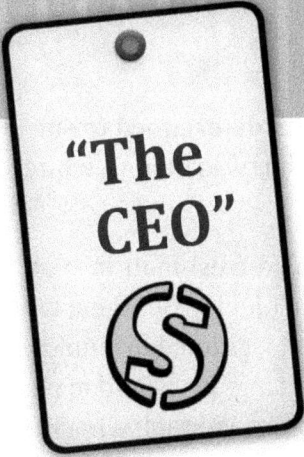

CHAPTER TWELVE

"The CEO" Ⓢ

JEF JON SIN

Nail It Before You Scale It—
Fans First, Expansion Later

> *With a self-penned world tour and a true "want it bad enough" attitude, Jef Jon Sin is a "no plan B" badass. From touring nonstop in a mobile recording studio he built himself, to piggybacking the biggest concerts in the nation to score new fans, Jef is all-in and extremely creative. Learn how he raised over $13,000 in three days on the crowdfunding site Kickstarter and tactics to build a die-hard tribe around you and your music.*

WHEN I FIRST STARTED, I WASN'T THINKING ABOUT MARKETING THE WAY I DO NOW. I was the only person who rapped in Benton, Kentucky, and that made me different. Being "different" has its pros and cons in this industry, obviously. But while my style of music made me stand out at the time, it also came with a lot of opposition. Some people didn't

get me. That didn't matter to me though. I was determined to succeed while staying true to who I am—and if that was being a white
rapper from Kentucky, so be it.

I started rapping in 2001 when I was 14 as a freshman in high
school with my best friend Seth Myers. I wasn't Jef Jon Sin then; we
were Ell and Will. Seth could play drums, banjo, guitar, harmonica,
violin, keyboard—he played it all, and he also sang. We would make
CDs at the house and sell them at our high school. We took what little resources we had and did all we could with them—an approach
that will serve you well when starting any business.

All we had was a Windows computer with an eight-track sequenc-
ing program called Acid. I didn't know anything about recording, so
honestly all the music sounded like shit. Mixing and mastering
wasn't something I understood at the time. We started with 100 CDs
and sold them for $5 each. Then we sold our CDs through movie
rental stores and a few CD stores. We sold the CDs for $15; we got
$10 and the stores got $5. We would take the initiative to think of
creative ways to get in front of people, a theme that has been the
common denominator of me making a full-time living through
music. We were always thinking outside the box. That movie rental
store was one of the most popular businesses for kids to hang out
at back then. And we wanted those kids to know who we were. I
went to the movie rental store and asked them to put the CD on the
counter. It was a cool, new extra revenue stream for them and increased exposure for us. When asking people to do anything for you,
you always have to think about how it's going to benefit them and
spin it that way. Even though we didn't make bank on this first
record, we started winning over the town and getting our name out
there. Building a loyal following, even a small one, can lead to making some pretty good foundational money.

In our sophomore year, we designed our next CD using a company in Canada, and although the music still wasn't mixed because we still didn't know what we were doing, the packaging looked amazing. Our junior year, in 2003, we made about $10,000 in three months with CD sales, since we had built that local fan base. There was a local teen club in my area that played our music every night. This helped my popularity and ability to sell my music in my area, and we would show up often, being present to connect with the people there and turn them into fans.

It's easier to get people in your hometown to like you first rather than spending a lot of money to get in front of people across the country who don't know you. People from your hometown are great for support; it's likely they'll want to see you succeed because they're proud you're from the same town they are. It's also easier to build a fan base locally since you can get in front of them on a regular basis. The one-on-one relationships and face-to-face conversations with those around you will start to create a buzz. Don't forget where you come from just because you have your eyes set on the fame and lifestyle you imagine in LA or Nashville or wherever it is. Look around, see who is there by you, and garner their support. *Nail it before you scale it.*

Don't Sign with Someone Just to be "Cool"

Around the same time my song was popular at the club in Benton, my cousin knew a guy named Reuben Nathan. Reuben was a concert promoter in London and handled a lot of big venues and booked some of the biggest acts in the world. He heard my music through my cousin and believed in me. Reuben was sold on how young I was with three CDs, a fan base, and bringing in money. The fact that I was a white rapper didn't hurt, either. That made me different. There weren't many back then! I signed my management agreement with him when I was 16, and he represented me for the next ten years.

Those couple years I had several other people who were interested in representing me, but I turned them down because we didn't connect. I wanted someone who was really willing to help. And I wanted someone "bigger" than me. Anything less I could handle on my own and not sign anything away. The saying "success is preparation meeting opportunity" couldn't be more true in this industry. That will always be the fact. I think having somebody represent you when you're in your teens is great if they believe in you and will sacrifice some of their time and money to put you where you need to be and to help you go all the way. It's about building a team of believers. Don't sign something with someone just because you think it makes you look cool or will advance your career. Make sure it will advance your career. Or you could really screw yourself up and be tied up when the right opportunity comes along. A manager who seeks you out, approaches you (because you've done the groundwork), and connects with you on all levels is a person worth spending your time with. You shouldn't have to ask someone to represent you; they should *want* to do it because they believe in you. Reuben was that person for me, and he was like a family member during that time.

Build Relationships Before You Ask for Favors

The first thing Reuben did for us was put us in a real studio. The next step, once the product was kick-ass, was going after labels. I was 19 and this was our first step into the real music business. It was also the first time I realized there is a whole community online for music, including forums and big pools of DJs to connect with. This was before YouTube, and we had seen somebody get 100,000 plays on their website and then get a record deal from having that many plays. Now it's the same process, just on a different site.

So I bought a website URL and focused a ton of energy on driving traffic and trying to expand our fan base. To get traffic to our new website, I spent hours talking to people in person and giving them business cards, on the phone with tastemakers, and in online forums, asking them to visit our website. No matter your genre, there are limitless amounts of people who don't know your music, so if you think you've got something great, it's OK to tell people about it. But this is important to understand: Don't be full of yourself and tell them "I've got the best shit in the world." No one likes spammers. And let's be honest, you're making a bad impression; people don't care because they don't know you, and you are a distraction. Nothing is in it for them! Tell them you respect what they do in the industry and you would love for them to check out what you have. That's respectful, strokes the ego, and then maybe they'll actually give your music a shot. I was able to network with many influential people online, and this is what helped me establish myself. It's a numbers game. You can reach out to thousands and get nothing in return. But it only takes one. Focus on building the relationship and not asking for something right away. Who likes that? No one. There is no such thing as overnight success in the music industry. It takes time to build relationships, and you never know when someone a few months or years from now will hook you up. But you have to have made a great impression.

No matter whom I contacted, either with a face-to-face conversation, call, or email, I followed up with them. I wanted people to know I was genuinely interested in them and not just trying to take their money or waste their time. With influencers, I checked in with them to see how they were and updated them every couple months to keep the relationship natural, as long as I was receiving mutual interest. That's how it works best 99 percent of the time.

Next Up: Music Business Degree

Ell and Will split up after five years, and Reuben continued managing my career as a solo artist. He launched FSH Records and secured an investor to help promote my project. We hired an independent record promoter and had a full-blown campaign for my single "Big Time." As the record gradually picked up spins across the country, representatives from every major record label contacted us showing interest. During all this, I also started a two-year bachelor's of music business degree at Full Sail University in Orlando, Florida, a creative arts school. It may sound odd to attend school at the same time we signed a record deal, but it's something I had always wanted to do.

Full Sail is where I met everybody I've worked with since, including my best friends and closest colleagues. An arts school can be a great choice, but it's up to you what you make of it. Some people go into it expecting to come out on the other end a great artist with all these connections, but it takes work, initiative, and putting yourself out there. The best thing that happened to me at Full Sail was the networking. I wanted to get a degree so I could get a good-paying job and promote my music no matter what, and Full Sail allowed me to surround myself with other like-minded creative people. If you choose an art school, don't get so self-absorbed or expect fame to be handed to you just because you're there and you're talented. So is everyone else. Pay attention to the people sitting next to you in class. Network! It's so important! Remember, this is a "who you know" business. Relationships are your most important tool. Find people you can work with to create content that will help you begin to build a stronger fan base.

While attending school, my radio campaign was in full swing. I even remember walking out of lectures to do national radio interviews. My life was really crazy during that time. As my record was growing on the radio and I was getting popular among the industry, I recognized that something was still wrong—I had no real fans. Other than the local buzz I had from grinding hand-to-hand in Kentucky, I had no real fans across the country. After the budget for the radio campaign dried up and the record wasn't in rotation anymore, it was obvious we had really made no impact. It didn't take long until the

PRO TIPS

GOING AT IT WITHOUT A LABEL

- *Do it yourself.* Don't rely on anyone to get it done for you; no one owes you anything. Even when you are paying someone to get something done for you, they are still not as invested as you are. Make sure you know exactly what you want, you can communicate it, and you can measure the results.

- *Trust your gut in everything.* If your gut is telling you to do it, then do it.

- *Set specific goals and work toward them.* Knowing and being able to communicate what you want is half the battle. When you are trying to make a living in the music business but have no plan, you are just a lost fish. Setting goals helps you stay on target for what's important.

major record labels that were calling when the record was spinning were not answering when the record stopped.

I met Travis Blackwell at Full Sail around this time. He was a graduate of the film program, and I saw some of his work at school. Travis was working on some great video content, so I introduced myself to him through Facebook. He wanted to build his video portfolio and I needed videos, so we collaborated. Finding someone to do this with was amazing. It happened pretty organically and wasn't forced. Making friends, doing what you love, and sharing a common vision with someone is the best part of this.

Trials, Errors, and Growth

Now that I had a professional videographer as one of my best friends, I had a real leg up on my competition. We shot many videos together in my last few months of school and then we moved to Los Angeles and were roommates. I was spending most of my time in LA working and trying to book shows. Honestly, LA was tough for me. I found myself spending all my days at work and stuck in traffic.

By this time, Reuben had been my manager for ten years; we had given it all we had and it was time to move on. Travis had introduced me to Bryce Stewart, who was a classmate of his at Full Sail. Bryce immediately showed interest in my project. He had been the manager of Yung Ro, a Houston-based rapper who was once signed to Chamillitary Entertainment. Bryce's background was in rap music and videography, a perfect fit for what I needed. He was young, hungry, and ready to work.

I've had to wear a lot of hats, but I don't mind. You have to as an independent artist. And I'm not scared of the work—I enjoy it. A lot of artists just want to handle the artistic side of things but don't want to handle the marketing that makes a business run. They want someone else to do it. You may luck out and find someone who believes in you like hell and will just do it. But for most, you have to know your own business. Know it inside and out. I know I'm willing to do things that other people aren't, and that has always given me an advantage and made me an attractive sell to people. I knew I wanted to work with somebody who understood the urgency I felt, and that's what really got me excited about Bryce. Bryce and I both wanted to meet new people and explore what could be created. We really clicked well together because it wasn't about the money, it was about making awesome art. He liked what I had built for myself, and I was lucky to find someone who wanted to be a part of it without expecting anything in return. We have become a true team.

We started to focus on playing live shows and break through in LA. I played House of Blues, Key Club, and some really cool venues, including private parties, but we just couldn't get a decent audience to stick and get momentum, no matter what we did. In LA, everybody wants to be famous; there are so many rappers, you have to have presales because the venues want you to pay $500 for an opening slot for some seedless singer. It was one wall hit after the other, and shows seemed like a letdown. But we didn't let this be the end of the line. A little setback shouldn't stop anyone. We decided to switch efforts and focus on our biggest strengths and take a different path. For some, I'd recommend pushing through if that's who you are and what makes you happy. But for me, I knew I would be miserable. I wanted to innovate.

One day Bryce called me and said, "Bro, we just need to go all-in." We decided to tour nonstop. An endless tour of getting out there and impacting people face to face. We had the product, we had our defining sound, and now we were ready to scale it.

Have Tricked-Out Van—Hit the Road

In 2012, we sold everything we had to buy an old FedEx Mercedes Sprinter Van—we named it The Ratoadskidmuffin—and we spent every dime we had turning this thing into a mobile studio, stage, and living space. We installed two fold-down beds inside and built our own cabinets. We put in two iMacs, everything we needed to record, a video editing bay, a roof-mounted stage, and a PA system so we could perform anywhere. This was our home, and the world was our stage.

A lot of people were really confused by the concept. Close family and industry mentors questioned us, but we knew it was what we had to do. If you know you have to do something, you can't let your mind or other people steer you in a false direction. You've got to stick to the plan. It may be wrong. But you won't know unless you try. And while some days and weeks were hard, connecting with people was the best part of the experience and built the strong connection to fans that we needed.

It wasn't as easy as it sounds, and wasn't as difficult as we made it. It took a lot of perseverance on our part to get the van totally designed and outfitted, but the rewards were instantly seen. Once it was ready to go, we took off, and immediately people were saying, "This is awesome! You've got the coolest van in the world. You are living the dream!" We're grateful our vehicle was so well received because we were able to use it as our platform to spread our music—and people remember us.

We had an iPad to collect email addresses in return for a free CD. That's one of the most viable promotional tactics we've ever done. We also put temporary tattoos of my name on people everywhere we performed. It takes creativity and innovation to get your name out and engage your fans. They have a million choices when listening to music. When you get your shot in front of people, make it something to remember. What makes you different?

We looked at major events that were coming to cities and markets we wanted to hit. We knew our target market (the people who liked music similar to ours). We'd be parked outside the arena as everyone was leaving, and I'd be on top of the van rapping or out in the crowd that formed around it. All the while Bryce was filming, tweeting, and talking to people, getting them engaged and making a connection. We got shut down by the cops almost every time, but it's that hustle and the crazy hype that gets people to remember us. And just like any relationship, we followed up on it and stayed in touch. Then we were off to the next major event where we could get in front of as many people as possible who we believed would love what we do.

Three Steps to Selling Merchandise

In between these guerilla performances, we toured with Nappy Roots. They are kind of like an extended family for me because nobody from Kentucky has really had much success with rap music except for them. Because I'm from Kentucky, too, they pulled for me to open for their shows. The day we hit the road with Nappy Roots, we had thirty-eight days booked in a forty-five-day period. It was thirty-eight shows in a row, and it was intense. We put so many miles on the van those weeks. We would drive to get to the next show, perform, sleep a little, and get to the next show.

We started to realize which techniques were the most effective to get people to buy merchandise. First, we had to be in front of the club every night because no one knew us. As people were walking in the door, we would hand them a wristband with my name on it and a free CD. And, of course, we'd get their email. As they entered the club and started to enjoy themselves, they might forget about the free merch, but once I hopped on stage to open for Nappy Roots, everyone was like, "Oh shit, that guy gave me a wristband!" So it got people interested when they remembered how nice I was to them. They paid attention to me on stage, and then after the show, they wanted to come meet me again. At that point, we would tell them that we have all this great stuff for sale. All told, it was a three-step process we implemented to connect with each audience. We made the most of every minute to get the attention of these fans, put tattoos on them, and make a connection.

I can't stress enough how important email addresses are. Even if we didn't sell anything to a lot of those people, it was important for us to collect their email at the beginning of the night. Now, we have a connection to them, and we stay in touch after that night. We make our emails interesting to them and *about* them. It's about making them like you as people too.

243

We took advantage of the whole five hours the club was open. And we tried to connect with as many people as we could during that time. We wanted to know them by the end of the night, and we wanted to sell our stuff, obviously. When you're an opener, it's important to find a way to make an impression on the audience. They might not initially be there to see you, but find a way to connect with them and you'll end up with many people heading to your merch stand at the end of the night.

Put in the effort you need to get live shows so you can start connecting with the people. For any opening slot I've ever had for a bigger act, I was contacted by each of the promoters because they had heard of us doing these pop-up shows in their cities and knew I could draw a crowd. The promoters pretty much run the city music-wise; if you're cool with one of them, it's easy to get gigs booked if they know you'll bring a crowd and they'll make money. It's about them, not you, when they're considering booking you. Promoters are easy to get in touch with as long as you don't try to reach them on the night of an event. They want to build relationships with people; that's their job. Offer to buy them a drink. Develop a relationship over time. It's a slow growth. Stay consistent and stay patient; these relationships can pay off big time.

Creating Other Revenue Streams

Aside from networking and learning how to connect with potential fans, I've been able to acquire a lot of skills that a normal artist wouldn't have. I'm able to edit my videos, and because I understand timing and rhythm as an artist, it improves the final product. Bryce is great at shooting and adding special effects to our videos, so he and I together can create amazing music videos and get big money for it by helping other artists who want the same quality. That's one avenue of income we choose to focus on. It's about capitalizing on each other's strengths and realizing where the most lucrative avenues are with the skills we have. People have come to expect great videos from us, and that is what they get. Basically you have to get out there and try to make it, and you have to be able to adjust to whatever circumstances come your way. Even while you're out there performing, you need to look at other streams of revenue besides just selling your own music and merchandise. What can you leverage with other artists and their fan base?

In addition to the extra income we get from creating videos for other artists, we have registered all our original music online with BMI. Doing this with our music on YouTube initially made us like $90; nothing crazy, but now that we have it registered, any time someone embeds it or streams it or whatever, the money comes directly to us since it's original content. It's just one small process that we took the time to do to ensure every penny would come to us. It's about finding a way to build your brand and make residual money for the future. YouTube has been great for that, and it is only getting stronger.

More important, no matter how music or technology evolves, you still need to go and touch people. Having your music on YouTube and getting views and additional income is important, but one hundred years from now, I don't know what the Internet is going to be like. What I do know is that a performer on stage with an audience will still draw a crowd. That live experience can't be replaced. Get in front of the people and let them connect with you face to face. If you're awesome online but suck live when those fans finally see you, you may not be able to retain them. A great live show takes practice and so does gaining confidence. There's no other way to do it besides just getting out there and doing it.

Independent vs. Label

I've been doing all this independently, and I personally like the independent route. Bryce and I spend all day focused on our goal. We want full control of everything. Taking initiative and learning everything on your own will really give you confidence, and you will know your business inside and out. I don't look at someone else to get stuff done for me because that leaves them in control of my life and my career. For me, the independent route makes the most sense. To us, dependency is the worst place we could be to stall progress. Others may choose to have a major label backing them, which may suit their skill sets better *if it's a good deal.* If a label is what you want, make sure you have your own thing going for you, rather than just letting the label invent who you are. For me, taking control of every aspect is motivating and challenging, which makes me a better businessperson and artist. I don't need a label for what I want to do. I just find a way to do it.

Sure everyone wants a good paycheck, but signing to a label or another entity is selling out your brand, so to speak. You are not in control of it. It's much better to have no deal than the wrong deal, and I think a lot of people don't understand that. They think, "If I can just get a shot, it will be perfect and I'll be a superstar." They don't see the caveats of signing away your brand before you really *have* a brand. Honestly, if I had nothing for the rest of my life but continued to inspire people every day and make a living doing what I love, I couldn't care less. That's my prerogative as an artist.

Kickstarter Done Right

As soon as it seemed like our routine was really working and generating income, our touring van was sideswiped and totaled in 2014. We had tons of equipment and hard drives that the insurance company didn't cover. We were in a really bad position because we had invested every nickel into it.

Running out of options, we launched a Kickstarter project. Since we already traveled across America and performed everywhere, we wanted to expand and take our brand overseas. We decided we were going to need $15,000 to pull off this next part of our tour. Kickstarter can be a great tool if you approach it correctly. As of writing this chapter, there are 701 active Kickstarter projects related to music alone, so if you want to tackle crowdfunding, you have to know how to make *your* project stand out and draw backers to successfully fund it. It is up to you to reach out, create a buzz about your project, and make it easy for people to want to contribute.

First, you can reach out to your family and close friends who are likely to want to help you reach your goal. I sent every contact in my phone a personal text message, followed by a personal call. I emailed and Facebook messaged everyone I thought would care. I asked people for just $1. It's easy for people to say yes to just $1, and often they would contribute more than that when they saw how passionate I was about the project and that I'd taken the time to personally reach out. That's a lot of work, but if you really want this, you have to be willing to earn it, not expect people to just hand over their hard-earned money to make *your* dream come true.

It's important to have a plan before diving in headfirst with fundraising. If you do most of the work in advance of launching your campaign, the money will come in faster and the process will be smoother. One way we took a lot of the heavy lifting out beforehand was drafting our email messages, text messages, Twitter messages, Facebook messages ahead of time. We then separated our lists into close friends, core fans, and those who were just acquaintances. We wrote personal messages to our close friends and core fans, but used a more mass-type of message for the others. Mass emails can be sent using sources such as FanBridge, or Google Chrome now has an extension that works with Gmail to schedule emails to send out on a certain day and a system that shows you who actually reads them.

On launch day, all you have to do is oversee the process rather than worrying about your wording and the content. You can quickly contact friends and fans, and be ready to respond and say thanks, rather than spend time writing several different posts when your project is already up and active. With that being said, *never* forget to say thank you. Say thank you to every person who contributes even just $1 to your project—and *personally* call them. "Thanks" says a lot. We found that when people noticed how much we appreciated them, they became more attached to our story and told their friends also. People will remember how gracious you were later down the road too.

To successfully fund your Kickstarter campaign, the biggest thing is to come up with a way to drive traffic to your project. Friends and family can go a long way, but you shouldn't stop there. Bloggers are an essential part of getting coverage for your campaign. Do your research and find bloggers who have readers who would potentially be interested in your campaign; find bloggers who are relevant and who have a great reach through their social media or email newsletters.

Look at Kickstarter projects that are similar to yours and do a search to see which blogs posted about their projects. A great resource for this is *www.compete.com.* You can enter any URL to see how many visitors the blogs get to their site each month; you don't need to pay for a plan to see simple statistics, which is all you really need. Bigger blogs aren't always better, but it's always nice to know how many people you can potentially reach on a site.

Also, you can "hack" Google by dropping a picture from a blog or article about any music project into the search bar at *images.google.com,* and you'll be shown a list of every website that has ever posted the image. Sort out the relevant ones you think would do a similar write-up on you and make a media list with a contact name, the publication, and the reach. These are the people you will contact to get publicity about your Kickstarter and who may show the most interest since they have written similar posts before.

Be aware that bloggers get a lot of stories pitched to them each day. Remember how I said you can reach out to your friends and family first? It's because they care about you and want to see you succeed. Make friends with bloggers as you pursue music. Care about what they do. Find out ways *you* can help *them.* Have conversations and form a friendship even if you aren't currently working on a Kickstarter. See why this would be helpful to do in advance? It's hard to build a relationship in 30 days, or the length of your campaign! Just like your friends and family who are happy to help you out by donating, your blogger friends will be happy to cover your project if you have an established relationship from showing them you care about their work, have been a follower of theirs, commented on their articles, etc.

Once your Kickstarter is up and running, don't forget to keep backers updated on your progress. Encourage sharing through social media, but don't send *too* many messages. Plan which days you will send emails to keep your backers engaged. The more people who share your link, the more potential backers will see your project.

In the end, I was very inspired by some of the encouraging messages we received and how many people wanted to see us continue. Through our efforts of reaching out to friends and simultaneously creating new friendships online, we ended up meeting our goal, and our Kickstarter was successfully funded. $13,000 of this funding came in just three days; it was incredible. Now we are in the middle of our European tour.

It really showed me that going for it, being all-in, is the only way to go—a lesson that I continually learn in this business. I hope that you also go for it, whatever is waking you up and reoccurring in your mind. I did, and just because of that, I succeeded and am making a successful living doing what I always wanted every single day. Feel free to contact me on any social media or through my website at *jefjonsin.com.* I would love to connect with you!

'Til next time,

I HANG OUT HERE

www.JefJonSin.com

Facebook: Facebook/
JefJonSin

Twitter: @JefJonSin

YouTube: YouTube.com/
JeffJohnsonTV

Instagram: @JefJonSin

RESOURCES

> *Here it is: some of our best tried and tested tools for at-taining not only a full-time living in the music industry but also for building a brand that is scalable and ready for the long haul. We've left out some of the obvious re-sources such as Facebook, Twitter, Instagram, Spotify, and SoundCloud; hopefully you're already rockin' there!*
>
> *We are confident that adding these resources to your arsenal will improve the size of your fan base and your wallet! They work...as long as you do! So get to clickin'!*

Books

All You Need to Know About the Music Business,
by Donald S. Passman

An incredible look at the modern music industry, this book has long been a leading resource for anyone looking to take their work in the music industry seriously.

howtheysellmusic.com/passman

"Any creative person who's considering working in the music business should read this book."

—Jimmy Iovine, chairman,
Interscope Geffen A&M Records

Anything You Want, by Derek Sivers

You want the dream musician lifestyle *and* creative freedom? Let me introduce you to Derek. He created CD Baby, the first online music store and distribution service for independent musicians. He then sold it for $22 million, but don't let us spoil the story of how he did it and why he loves helping musicians succeed. We'll let him speak for himself.

howtheysellmusic.com/sivers

The Craft of Lyric Writing, by Sheila Davis

Commonly known as the "Songwriting Bible," this book is packed with information to teach you *why* hit songs are hit songs and how to craft your music with complete commercial potential.

howtheysellmusic.com/lyricwriting

"Now I know what to say to young lyricists who come to me for advice: Buy The Craft of Lyric Writing. *It's all there."*
—Sheldon Harnick,
Pulitzer Prize Lyricist, "Fiddler on the Roof"

4-Hour Workweek, by Tim Ferriss

As an artist in the spotlight, you can't just improve on your music alone. Personal development is integral to your success in every aspect of your life. A book that stays on Amazon's best-seller's list year after year, Tim Ferriss teaches you how to get out of the 9 to 5 and redesign your life on your own terms. *A must read!*

howtheysellmusic.com/tim

Guerilla Music Marketing, by Bob Baker

There really aren't enough words to describe how valuable Bob Baker's wisdom is. From his podcast to his books, his words are prolific and tested, and a valuable resource whether you are a novice or a music industry expert.

howtheysellmusic.com/bobbaker

Jab, Jab, Jab, RIGHT HOOK, by Gary Vaynerchuck

You want to stand out from the newsfeed on social media? Gary gets it down to a science to take back control of your content and audience, complete with case studies of the most successful posts and why they worked. And, of course, what *you* can do to be equally as visible online as some of the biggest brands in the world.

howtheysellmusic.com/garyv

Music Success in Nine Weeks, by Ariel Hyatt

Ariel guides you through how to tackle some of the toughest problems in marketing to your online audience. In a nine-week, step-by-step course, you will watch your business and your music reach more fans than you thought possible in just under three months.

howtheysellmusic.com/hyatt

The $150,000 Music Degree, by Rick Barker

Taylor Swift's former manager and now a private consultant, there is little Rick *doesn't* know about the music industry. Sit back and unpack this baby, and be ready to be transformed.

howtheysellmusic.com/rickbarker

Career/Financial Management

ASCAP

A wonderful PRO. You've created music you're extremely proud of—now you need to protect it. ASCAP, short for the American Society of Composers, Authors and Publishers, is a phenomenal resource and guide to licensing your work and protecting the rights of fellow artists and creators.

howtheysellmusic.com/ascap

BMI

To get recognized and paid, at some point, every songwriter must join a performing rights organization (PRO)—and a great one at that. BMI will provide you with a wealth of knowledge that is crucial to your success. From news to advocacy and advice for your career, BMI's got you covered.

howtheysellmusic.com/bmi

SESAC

SESAC is another PRO option. SESAC will not only allow you to learn to mindfully protect your music and original work, but will advise you on the ins and outs of how to conduct your business, while keeping you networked with some extremely talented songwriters.

howtheysellmusic.com/sesac

SoundExchange

Make sure you're getting paid the royalties you deserve and sign up for an account today. The site educates and informs on topics ranging from copyright to licensing and is a must for anyone who is actively releasing music. Trust us.

howtheysellmusic.com/soundexchange

Crowdfunding

Indiegogo

Another popular crowdfunding platform. Expose your creativity to the world and get funding from people who believe in it.

howtheysellmusic.com/indiegogo

Kickstarter

Fund hundreds of projects that others are dreaming of or get funding for your own. The most popular of the fundraising sites.

howtheysellmusic.com/kickstarter

Patreon

Patreon lets fans support their favorite creators by becoming patrons. Unlike other fundraising services, which raise for a single big event, Patreon is ongoing fan-funding for creators who create a stream of smaller works.

howtheysellmusic.com/patreon

PledgeMusic

Keep up with the timelines of those you love to listen to. PledgeMusic provides up-to-date notifications about the latest productions of your favorite artists and music, and is a way to fund projects that are specific to music. What could be better?

howtheysellmusic.com/pledgemusic

Informative Websites and Blogs

BLOGS

The [DIY] Musician

The site designed for do-it-yourself musicians, like us, provides resources that are extremely helpful to artists who are aiming to create their careers on their own. Seeing a recurring theme here?

howtheysellmusic.com/diy

HypeBot

Knowledge is power, right? Well, HypeBot merges your knowledge of both music business and music technology. Come on, you know you need more brilliant coffee shop discussion topics.

howtheysellmusic.com/hypebot

Music Industry How To

With Music Industry How To, Shaun Letang informs his readers and community on how to develop their business in the most efficient way possible. If you're gonna keep a handful of blogs in your wallet, let's just say this is your Benjamin, baby.

howtheysellmusic.com/howto

WEBSITES

Music Industry Blueprint

Marketing specialist Rick Barker has worked in the music industry for years, having springboarded the careers of artists from Taylor Swift to Sugarland, and now he wants to help you. Through his industry insight featured on Music Industry Blueprint, Barker sheds light on the sometimes challenging and murky how-tos of the business.

howtheysellmusic.com/blueprint

Music Starts Here

With an emphasis on marketing and branding techniques, Music Starts Here is run in Nashville and provides some incredible information. Basically, they're great at holding your hand through the process of getting started and taking yourself to the next level.

howtheysellmusic.com/musicstartshere

Music Strategy Courses and Online Vocal Coaching

MUSIC STRATEGY COURSES

Music Marketing Manifesto

After scoring one of the largest new artist deals of all time, and *still* being dropped from the label, John Oszajca began studying Internet marketing to sell his albums. Over $2 million later, he shows artists how to create the same system to build a fan base and sell albums using the Internet. Bingo!

howtheysellmusic.com/mmm

New Artist Model

Learn how to take your creativity and create multiple income streams. It's all here: from finding sponsors and publishing deals to booking more gigs and starting your own label. Dave Kusek is a marketing genius.

howtheysellmusic.com/newartistmodel

Social Media House

With her proven and trackable one-of-a-kind system, Ariel Hyatt shows artists how to score big using social media marketing. Ariel is a highly sought-after speaker for helping artists break into the industry and make a huge splash on a budget.

howtheysellmusic.com/socialmediahouse

VOCAL COACHING

Judy Rodman

If you can't make it to take a lesson from celebrity coach Judy Rodman personally, well, we feel sorry for you. But don't freak out: You can get her "Singing in the Studio" course online! When you're paying anywhere from $1,500 to $6,000 for a radio-ready master recording, you can't afford not to nail it in the studio. Judy shows you how to sing in the studio like the best of them and the techniques that differ from the stage. Go Judy!

howtheysellmusic.com/judy

Ken Tamplin

Vocal coach to the stars, Ken is a close friend to several of the artists in the book. Ken is a master at technique and teaching you to dominate any vocal styling your heart desires. We are huge fans of Ken's, and he offers several different ways to work with him, including videos and DVDs, and even Skype lessons. Take a look at some of his free tutorials too!

howtheysellmusic.com/ken

Singorama

Another good online course with professional songwriting tips and tricks to improve your melody selection, structure, and abilities to craft unique, marketable songs that are sure to stand out.

howtheysellmusic.com/singorama

The Superior Singing Method

Aaron Anastasi walks you through online modules that are focused on building range and maintaining control of your voice. We tend to like those things.

howtheysellmusic.com/superiorsinging

Tom Jackson's Onstage Success

You have a great voice, but how are you as a performer? Touring is where you make 90 percent of your revenue as a musician, so you need to be top notch. A coach for stars like Taylor Swift, Katy Perry, and Jars of Clay, Tom Jackson coaches you how to create moments for your audience and an experience they will not soon forget.

howtheysellmusic.com/tomjackson

Opportunities

CrucialMusic

Crucial is a place for artists, label reps, and music supervisors to connect. They have a very simple submission process to get your music to the decision-makers you need to get the placements that you want.

howtheysellmusic.com/crucial

Music Clout

Opportunities on top of opportunities...oh, and community. Basically, you need to be here.

howtheysellmusic.com/musicclout

Musicpage

Create a profile for your own exposure, then learn from the profiles of other artists. A great place to submit music for licensing. A couple of our artists have gotten the majority of their licensing deals from this site alone.

howtheysellmusic.com/musicpage

Music Xray

21st Century A&R. We like this. Build your artist profile and submit to industry opportunities. Music Xray has the most industry engagement of any platform online.

howtheysellmusic.com/musicxray

Taxi

Long story short, Taxi helps independent artists, songwriters, and composers get record, publishing, and film/TV deals. Be a good samaritan and get your music to the people who need it.

howtheysellmusic.com/taxi

Promotion, Distribution, and Artist Tools

ArtistGrowth

If you need help organizing the *business* of your music, check out ArtistGrowth software, the ultimate business management tool. With tools that help you plan and track everything from finances to event scheduling, AG ensures that everything you need to maintain your brand and career runs smoothly. After all, if you don't take care of the revenue, you can't have a healthy career!

howtheysellmusic.com/artistgrowth

BandCamp

BandCamp essentially draws together a collection of the hottest acts in music, allowing music fans to sample and discover emerging acts they may be interested in. What we think is one of the most valuable and well-recognized resources available to artists, BandCamp divides albums based on genre, facilitating search and discovery of new records. BandCamp will undoubtedly increase your exposure and aid in future success!

howtheysellmusic.com/bandcamp

Bandsintown

If you're a musician, you know the value of live music and the exposure it can lead to. You also undoubtedly understand the importance of having a strong social media following to further ensure this exposure. The Bandsintown app allows fans to stay in the loop with what their favorite musical acts are up to, keeping both the artist and their supporters happy.

howtheysellmusic.com/bandsintown

Buffer

Buffer helps you pre-schedule your posts to your social media accounts with one click. Buffer is a Google Chrome extension, so if you see something you want to tweet, it's possibly the easiest thing you'll do all day.

howtheysellmusic.com/buffer

CD Baby

The first and best music store on the web, ladies and gentlemen. CD Baby has always been on the top of the indie music game. Looking to get your song on iTunes, Spotify, Amazon, Beats, etc? Want to sell your music from your own web store? Want to discover new music? Look no further!

howtheysellmusic.com/cdbaby

Digital Delivery Services

A digital distribution service based out of Nashville, we prefer DDS for customized help in the strategic marketing for your single, EP, or album. Don't just put it up for sale. Make *a plan* to increase your sales and visibility on iTunes, and offer your music globally. DDS can provide career guidance and help get your foot in the door with many other Nashville services.

howtheysellmusic.com/digitaldelivery

Fiverr

Fiverr is your marketplace for services starting at just $5. From graphic design and lyric videos to blogging and radio promotion, we aren't saying this is your one-stop-shop, but it could be. Be sure to read reviews and check for quality, but Fiverr is one incredibly helpful tool for anyone on a budget.

howtheysellmusic.com/fiverr

Free New Tune

"How do I get my music heard?" It's probably the biggest problem independent artists face. Free New Tune offers a solution by helping artists set up a three-tier benefit system for fans who share their content. All fans have to do to get exclusive perks from an artist is to enter their email. A viral component is added by letting fans share the content to win bigger and better prizes. The more friends they get to download the tune, the faster they can reach each prize tier, rewarding fans for sharing the music they love. When done right, this template has garnered as many as 58,000 email addresses from new fans within a single week.

howtheysellmusic.com/freenewtune

ReverbNation

ReverbNation helps growing artists by introducing them to industry partners, exposing them to fans, and giving them the promo tools to help them grow. Create your profile, upload your music, and start climbing your hometown's Reverb chart!

howtheysellmusic.com/reverbnation

Thunderclap

Wanna go viral? Thunderclap is similar to fundraising, but instead of raising funds, you're raising people's commitment to post to social media. In other words, if 500 people commit to tweeting about your new album, at the end date, all 500 will automatically send out a social media post about your album at the same time, making that viral dream of yours a reality. Nice.

howtheysellmusic.com/thunderclap

TweetAdder

Want more followers on Twitter? TweetAdder has been around for a while and knows the game, *and* can automate your process for following, unfollowing, and communicating with your target audience. It doesn't get any better than this.

howtheysellmusic.com/tweetadder

Virool

Want to go viral on YouTube but don't have the time? Allow Virool to automate the process *and* stay within YouTube's terms of services. They get your video in front of customized publishers and targeted viewers to completely maximize the eyeballs that see your video.

howtheysellmusic.com/virool

Website Analytics, Email, and Design

ANALYTICS

DemographicsPro

Curious about your Twitter following? DemographicsPro has your answer. This easy-to-use site allows you to analyze the activity on and related to your Twitter page so you can more effectively market to your target audience.

howtheysellmusic.com/demographics

Iconosquare

As Instagram becomes more popular, it is becoming an increasingly useful marketing tool. Iconosquare will answer all your questions related to how your page is doing, providing a chance for you to increase activity, business, exposure, and eventual success.

howtheysellmusic.com/iconosquare

Next Big Sound

Want to be successful in the pursuit of the music business? Of course, you do! That's why you need to look into Next Big Sound. With analytics, tips, and tricks for your entire career and digital footprint, NBS will help you make the best next step to move your following and business forward.

howtheysellmusic.com/nextbigsound

EMAIL

AWeber

Remember that all-important email list? AWeber is the top of the line as far as monitoring your numbers, fan conversions, and sales, and keeping yourself organized. Email is your direct-to-fan foundation, and AWeber is the best around.

howtheysellmusic.com/aweber

FanBridge

This easy-to-navigate site does exactly what its name implies: bridges the artist to the fans. Not only does it help you use email and social media to your advantage, but it connects you to fans in a way you can communicate with them on your terms.

howtheysellmusic.com/fanbridge

WEBSITE DESIGN

Bombplates

Want an awesome-looking website specifically tailored to musicians? Of course, you do. You need Bombplates. This site allows you to design refreshing websites that are both aesthetically pleasing and easily navigable. And did we mention it was built for artists?

howtheysellmusic.com/bombplates

DesignPickle

DesignPickle gives you unlimited amounts of graphic design work each month for $195.00. Album art? Business cards? Website graphics? Banners? You can get it all for just $195 a month with unlimited revisions, next business day turnaround, and the ability to cancel anytime! Even if you just want it for one month. Incredible! Use our promo code "isellmusic" at checkout to get 25% off!

howtheysellmusic.com/designpickle

99designs

From business cards to logos, websites to mobile apps, 99designs has everything you could possibly need to create for your business. You put your design need up on the site and set what you are willing to pay for it. You get *tons* of unique designs submitted, then you pick the winner who gets paid for it.

howtheysellmusic.com/99designs

Wix

Arguably the easiest website creator ever. Gone are the days when you have to spend hundreds or even thousands on a socially acceptable and competitive website. Wix is verifiably heaven-sent.

howtheysellmusic.com/wix

For more information and resources visit

howtheysellmusic.com

or for ordering information contact

holler@howtheysellmusic.com

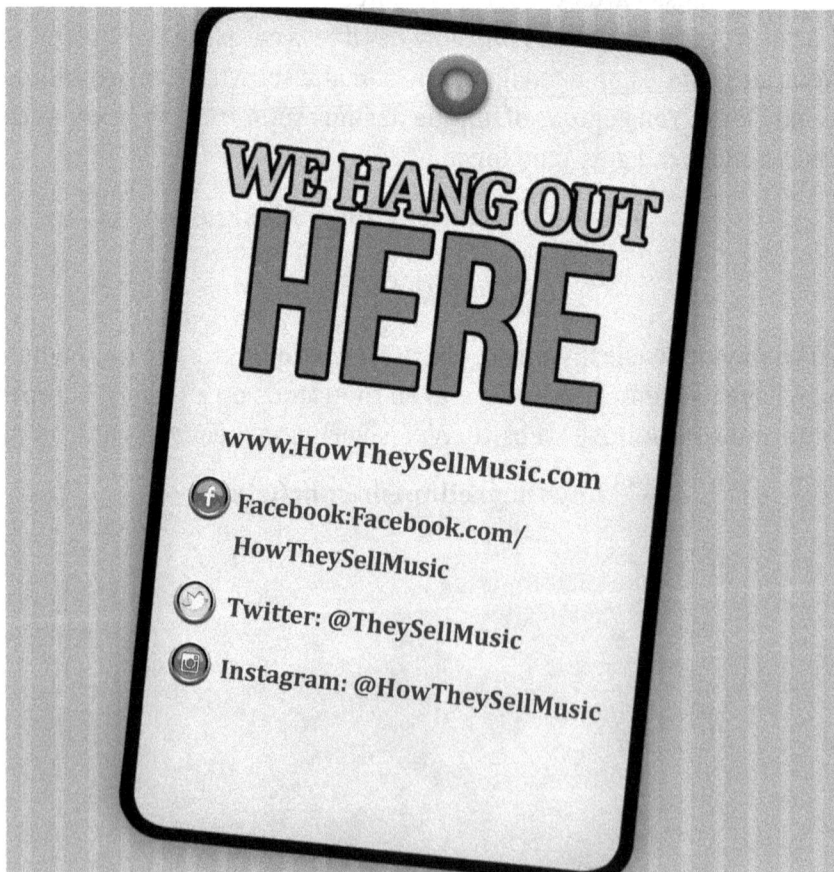

www.ingramcontent.com/pod-product-compliance
Lightning Source LLC
Chambersburg PA
CBHW060009050426
42448CB00012B/2674